[handwritten: Thank you John for all you do for Colorado in your library to the Conservative message God Bless, Allen Unruh]

THE POLITICALLY INCORRECT BOOK OF HUMOR

WHY IT'S BETTER TO BE RIGHT THAN POLITICALLY CORRECT

[handwritten: Website : @MakeAmericaLaughAgain.com]

DR. ALLEN UNRUH

THE POLITICALLY INCORRECT BOOK OF HUMOR

WHY IT'S BETTER TO BE RIGHT THAN POLITICALLY CORRECT

World Ahead Press is a division of WND Books. The views and opinions expressed in this book are those of the author and do not necessarily reflect the official policy or position or WND Books.

Paperback ISBN: 978-1-944212-20-9
eBook ISBN: 978-1-944212-21-6

Printed in the United States of America
16 17 18 19 20 21 LSI 9 8 7 6 5 4 3 2 1

DEDICATION

I dedicate this book to my wife Leslee. Every man's dream is to marry up, and I've been blessed. Leslee has the charm of Princess Di, the compassion of Mother Teresa, and the courage of Joan of Arc. I asked her if she will still love me when I'm old, fat, and ugly. She said, "I still do, don't I?" She has nicknamed me Columbo, and she has learned to just laugh at my limitless imperfections.

I also dedicate it to our grandkids whose favorite words are: "Papa, tell me a joke."

ENDORSEMENTS

Want to sound clever, at the top of your game and the smartest person in the room? It's simple. Read, remember, and repeat some of my friend, Dr. Allen Unruh's thousands of one-liners. Your friends will wonder how you got so smart, so quick.
—*Richard A. Viguerie, Chairman, American Target Advertising*

My dear friend, Dr. Allen Unruh, has a talent that only God could give. In his book he will make you laugh, cry and deeply pierce your heart, all at the same time. The Politically Incorrect Book of Humor illustrates irony and truth like no other book. Dr. Unruh speaks boldly and without compromise all wrapped in a blanket of laugh-out-loud humor. I highly recommend this book to everyone for its' insightful wisdom and truth written on every page.
—*Dick Bott Sr., Bott Radio Network, Founder and Board Chairman*

Dr. Allen Unruh is the personification of Mozart's quote, "True genius lies in simplicity." At the same time, there is profound wisdom in his words. Dr. Unruh is a man with the truth, who arms the reader so the person has the Power of an Army. On each subject, you will be equipped to respond to the leftists with simple, laser-like answers, leaving the individual speechless.

—*Somers H. White, CPAE, FIMC, Speaker Hall of Fame, 3,000 paid speeches in all 50 states and on 6 Continents, Former Arizona State Senator and Bank President*

My stomach always hurts from laughter after chatting with Allen. He has phenomenal insight into politics – and incredible way of expressing it with humor. The Politically Incorrect Book of Humor is a must read. Sometimes it's best to learn harsh realities with a good laugh.

—*Josh D. McDowell, Author, Communicator*

The sage of South Dakota will keep you laughing and smiling at each turn of the page as he delivers razor sharp political zingers. It is good medicine for those ill with political correctness.

—*Michael Y. Warder, Senior Fellow, Pepperdine University School of Public Policy*

Dr. Allen Unruh is the Mark Twain of the conservative movement and that's OK with me.

—*Jim Gilmore, President of Free Congress and Presidential Candidate*

Allen Unruh has assembled a veritable encyclopedia of conservative one-liners. The Politically Incorrect Book of Humor has enough puns, barbs, digs, snappy comebacks and flat-out funny jokes to spice up hundreds of speeches. Comedy is cruel, but the humor here is warm and bright. If you can get through even

half a page without laughing out loud, you must be a sour feminist or some other humorless creature in need of a funny bone transplant.
—*Robert Knight, Author, Columnist*

Political correctness is a disease. America needs a Doctor to fix it! Dr. Allen Unruh to the rescue with some great laughs in his The Politically Incorrect Book of Humor. Donald Trump is proud of the good Dr.!
—*Scott Hennen, Host, What's On Your Mind Radio Show, Partner, Flag Family Media*

Allen's book The Politically Incorrect Book of Humor tickles your funny bone and imparts wisdom. That's a win-win for any reader.
—*Dick Patten, American Business Defense Council, Washington D.C*

I have laughed until it hurt reading Allen's social, surprisingly pointed and unnervingly correct politically incorrect one-liners!!! Allen has been gifted with wit and skill at once nuanced and hilarious. What a combination. Enjoy!!!
—*Judith Gelernter Reisman, PhD, Author, Research Professor, Liberty University School of Law*

One of the greatest threat to America's future is political correctness. It has stifled our First Freedom and left Americans fearful that PC police will swoop at any moment. Dr. Unruh's book, The Politically Incorrect Book of Humor provides those who are tired of the assault on American values a weapon to fight back

with – humor! Humor is a universal language and The Politically Incorrect Book of Humor is a not so secret, secret weapon to defend the principles of liberty.
—*Tony Perkins, President, Family Research Council*

This book is proof that conservatives have a great sense of humor and are not dour, long faced serious people as so often caricatured in the media. Allen Unruh's own wit and playfulness is evident on every page. He's known in the movement as a master jokester and from now on will be known as a master literary humorist as well!
—*Colin Hanna, Let Freedom Ring*

People who disagree with the left are called racists, bigots, homophobes, intolerant right wing extremists. This strategy is to silence the opposition by intolerant, politically correct, anti-Christian bigots. Now, at last, a book that uses humor to expose liberal lunacy for what it is. Dr. Unruh's thousands of one-liners cut through the maze of confusion. If the left won't laugh, they can live on Prozac.
—*Stu Epperson Sr., Salem Communications.*

I just finished reading through Dr. Allen Unruh's new work, The Politically Incorrect Book of Humor. It should be required reading for every concerned American, regardless of political stripe. I laughed the entire read. Dr. Unruh is one of the most serious minded and effective Conservatives I know...but he has enough confidence in the rightness of his positions and enough determined wisdom to be able to laugh a little while he fights the good fight.

—*Pastor Rick Scarborough, Vision America*

Dr. Unruh's book, The Politically Incorrect Book of Humor reveals why easy street leads to a dead end. Utopia is a word meaning: NOWHERE! In the world of the insane, normal people are considered NUTS. Now you can have the strongest weapon – words that will stop the left dead in their tracks.

—*Troy Newman, President, Operation Rescue*

It doesn't take a genius or even an IQ of one's shoe size to figure out that Allen Unruh has a particular gift... and it's a gift that affects those around him in a pleasant way. He has the gift of looking at life in a humorous way and it shows.... Everyone reading his latest book will enjoy every minute of it.

—*David Noebel, Founder, Summit Ministries*

This fun book will be useful to anyone who likes to entertain as well as inform his listeners...as a speaker or conversationalist. A smiling and laughing audience is more receptive to any message and this book provides ammunition to bring smiles and laughter to any audience...... Dr. Unruh has a gift for making people laugh. In this book he passes that gift on the rest of us.

—*Don Hodel*

Allen is a naturally funny guy and his book arranges that wit and the many one-liners by subject matter. It's

a good read for any conservative wanting to collect wit and one-liners for use in the future.
—*Kelly Shackelford, Liberty Institute*

It's a good thing Allen Unruh is a Chiropractor because after reading his book I am doubled over from laughing.
—*Cal Thomas, Syndicated and USA Columnist/Fox News Contributor*

The left succeeds far too often in squelching serious debate by using political correctness to silence the opposition. It's time to take its influence down a notch. Dr .Allen Unruh does this beautifully in his new book, The Politically Incorrect Book of Humor.
—*Penna Dexter, Cohost, nationally syndicated Point of View Radio Show*

The unparalleled wit and wisdom of Unruh! Thank you, Allen, for this valuable resource to add some spice to my sermons! I recommend it as a handy addition for any public speaker's library.
—*Paul K. Blair, Pastor, Fairview Baptist Church, President, Reclaiming America for Christ*

Allen Unruh is brilliant! He has the wit of Shakespeare with the ability to condense complicated issues into understandable, humorous anecdotes and sage axioms! He is a true genius!
—*William J. Federer, Author and Speaker*

Dr. Allen Unruh brings the ongoing drivel of political correctness to a screeching halt and conveys pivotal truths with humor that readers will not soon forget. It is a privilege to have a new round of his wit and wisdom to share around the dinner table. Dr. Unruh keeps you laughing and learning.

—*Curtis Bowers, Author and producer of documentaries Agenda and Agenda 2*

The curse of our age is political correctness. It is liberal censorship before a word is spoken. How refreshing to find a book with clean humor that dares to be politically incorrect. Dr. Allen Unruh has provided a great service in giving us a book filled with one-line zingers that can be shared in public.

—*Jerry Newcombe, DMin, On-air personality/Senior Producer*

Allen's new book, The Politically Incorrect Book of Humor, is a must read for everyone. Specifically, it will be an invaluable tool for speech writers and pundits alike who are engaged in the world of politics. Humor is an essential part of any communication aimed at engaging an audience. This book deserves a spot on your bookshelf. Cheers.

—*Sally Pipes, President and CEO, Pacific Research Institute*

Thanks to Allen for doing the hard work so readers can have all the fun. I couldn't stop laughing. Groucho Marx said, "Politics is the art of looking for trouble, finding it everywhere, diagnosing it incorrectly and applying the wrong remedies." Allen has triumphed in doing the opposite. More Please.

—*Colby May, Esq., Director and Senior Counsel, American Center for Law and Justice, Washington Office,*

Never have I read a book with so much timeless truth coupled with so much relevant humor. Once I started to read it, I simply couldn't put it down!
—*Brad Dacus President, Pacific Justice Institute*

Dr. Allen Unruh is brilliant and is inspired by grace to skewer the foibles of a fallen and pretentious culture. He is funny and worth enjoying. That said, I have not had time to read his book, but I do endorse Allen, himself.
—*Ted Baehr, Movieguide*

I heartily endorse Dr. Allen Unruh's book of humor attacking the pure sickness, weakness and stupidity of "Political Correctness" and the "Fear of Mankind." This book will be a healthy tonic for those who live in the real world and useful to them for pointing out the idiocy of political liberalism, socialism, and atheism.
—*Jay Grimstead, Director of Coalition on Revival*

When Dr. Allen Unruh speaks with my Political Science classes. My students, of all political persuasions, discover that his relentless humor actually conveys the most seriously thought-provoking commentary they will hear about politics in America today. Our biggest problem is not political differences but political indifference, and nobody reading his latest book can remain indifferent.
—*Marshall Damgaard, Professor of Political Science, University of South Dakota*

Now anyone can enjoy the quick wit and humor of Allen Unruh. We all know that humor brightens our day

and Allen is a constant beam of sunshine. I thoroughly enjoyed his book and I'm sure you will too.
—*Bradley Mattes, President, Life Issues Institute*

Thank you so much Dr. Unruh, for sharing your vast resource of humor on almost every political subject. The profound wit and wisdom in this book fills a huge vacuum when most people are mad at the direction this great country is going. Like the sizzle that sells the steak, Allen's humor sells America like nothing I have ever read.
—*Jim Martin, President, 60 Plus Foundation*

Humor is a universal language in every country. It is a vital part of communication. When Robin Williams and Joan Rivers died, at the Grammy's they played some of their old jokes from 20 years ago and the crowd was aghast because their jokes were not politically correct. The left created the right not to be offended, a right not in the Bill of Rights.
—*Dr. Ken Campbell*

Allen Unruh brings levity and light to politics. Conservatives (and even liberals) looking for laughs will enjoy this book.
—*Tom Fitton, Judicial Watch*

Dr. Unruh and I hardly agree on anything politically, but I have belly laughs every time he comes to my restaurant for lunch. I highly recommend this book to everyone who enjoys humor in politics.
—*Former U.S. Senator Jim Abourezk, SD*

Amidst the rancor of competing views and political opponents, Dr. Allen Unruh's book is a breath of fresh air. He writes as he speaks with an incredible sense of humor in which he visualizes and articulates thoughts that will make anyone laugh and yet think about ideas he conveys. . . . . Every page of this book you read will make you want to get to the next one to see what gems you will experience. The book is a masterpiece of humor that carries with it powerful gems of thought and persuasion. Thank you, Dr. Unruh

—*Mat D. Staver, Esq., Founder and Chairman, Liberty Counsel, Offices in DC, FL, and VA*

Allen has a great sense of humor and knows how to use it to get far more than a laugh!

—*Dr. Raymond McHenry Pastor, Westgate Memorial Baptist Church Beaumont, Texas Founder and Editor, In Other Words*

Conservatives already have the best sense of humor, and this book proves it. While Allen Unruh is not politically correct, and neither am I, why not enjoy the process? I've known Dr. Unruh for years and I endorse this book.

—*State Rep. Klingenschmitt, PhD, Colorado.*

Dr. Unruh is an outstanding humorist and I'm sure glad he's on our side. I highly recommend this book.

—*Jeff Myers, President Summit Ministries.*

Dr. Unruh is the Johnny Carson of the conservative movement. This book is a must-read to break the chains of political correctness that stifles human thought.

—*Lew Uhler, President, National Tax Limitation committee.*

CONTENTS

INTRODUCTION

1. I was born in a one-room shack, in a one-horse town. I went to a one-room school house. I read the book, *The Power of One* and started studying one-liners. That's because I can't remember two.

2. I went to school to develop my wit. Unfortunately I only attended half the classes. But it's still better than a dim-wit or a nit-wit. I guess when I die I'll be at my wit's end. Winston Churchill said, "Wit is a sword." "It is meant to make people feel the point as well as to see it." It is the salt of conversation, not the food. I was invited to be in "Who's who?" And to be in who's who, you have to know what's what.

3. Finally, a book that articulates how politics and public policy affects every day Americans. There are hundreds of one-liners, and jokes that can be used in speeches to make a point, or simply to help you scintillate your everyday conversation. The gift of humor may be one of the most important gifts you can give to your friends and family. Words are the most powerful drug of mankind.

4. Times are getting tough, and who doesn't have stress? The other day I called dial-a-prayer and they put me on hold. I lined up our youngest daughter once with a standup comic. He never showed up. You might say she was stood up by a stand up.

5. In this information age, one of the greatest needs is for organized information. I believe the right words can be worth 1000 pictures. The right phrases or one-liner on key issues can make your point quickly and if it's accompanied with humor it dramatizes your purpose. The one-liner moves with a snap and a sizzle that creates a sense of spontaneity lacking in stories. It is the humor of today. Now you can flavor your ideas with wisdom and humor. The way to a person's heart is through their funny bones. This book is chalk full of material for politicians, preachers, public speakers, and people of principle who want the right joke, anecdote, or quote to drive home a point. Comedy is a craft. The techniques used to make people laugh are generally not known. It takes long painful years to develop.

6. Words mean things. We live in an age when foreign philosophies have redefined the meaning of words, or demonized words in the name of political correctness. Political correctness has resulted in confusion of thoughts in this generation. There is so much information overload, I saw a bumper sticker that said, "Honk if you believe in anything." But certain truths transcend time. Too many old truths have been forgotten or never learned. George Orwell said, "The further a nation drifts from truth, the more hated the people are who speak truth to power. I've been careful to select from my own humor files pithy material on relevant topics. Not all of the humor is original, much of it is, and a

lot is a result of re-wording statements to make it humorous.

7. This book is not written to make everyone a standup comedian. But it can be a tremendous resource for anyone who wants to influence with every day conversation or in giving speeches to drive home a point. Humor is contagious. With this book, you can be a carrier.

8. Since 1970 I have been collecting one-liners, quips, stories and quotes to spice up communication. After reading thousands of books and underlining them with their key points, a philosophy and worldview forms that gives a sense of purpose.

9. To remember the right one-liner it became important to categorize them into a series that can be imbedded in the recesses of your mind. To articulate a worldview it's vital to be able to make your point in a way that relates to the average person. Laughing is the shortest distance between two people.

10. Using humor is a vital part of communication. Ronald Reagan had a debate with Walter Mondale for president of the United States. Reagan was the oldest candidate to ever run for president. When the issue of age came up it was thought to be a gotcha question. America is not ready for some old, out of date duffer to run the country. But Ronald Reagan was ready and said, "I have vowed to not make age an issue in this campaign. I refuse to exploit, for political purposes, the youth and inexperience of my opponent." The crowd, along with Mondale,

roared. When interviewed by the mainstream media afterwards, Mondale said, "At that moment, I knew I had lost the election."

11. How important is humor in politics? Humor is serious business. The use of humor can disarm your opponent more than any form of communication.

12. The use of humor is exaggeration, insults, and sometimes a play on words. However, the right to not be offended now is superior to all other rights. Where did that right ever come from? Two of America's most famous comedians Robin Williams and Joan Rivers both died in the same year. At the next Grammies they paid tribute to them by playing back some of their jokes they had told 20-30 years ago. The crowd was aghast because most of their jokes were no longer politically correct. Almost everyone was offended at something they said. So I have decided to be an equal opportunity offender. If you are offended, get over it. Lighten up. Life is too short. It's time to smile at ourselves and enjoy our differences.

13. This book is written to address a wide variety of issues with renewed perspective.

ABORTION

1. I have to march because my mother didn't have the right to have an abortion."
   Rep. Maxine Waters (D-CA), in response to a Washington Times reporter asking why she was marching at a Planned Parenthood Rally.
2. I've noticed that 100% of the people who advocate for abortion rights have already been born.
   Ronald Reagan
3. Nobody says, "Oh no, I just killed my appendix."
4. A liberal said, "I hate the word KILL; rather say, we will terminate the pregnancy." It's much more palatable than saying we need to kill the baby inside the womb. Would he say, "Let's kill the crabgrass," or would it sound better to TERMINATE the crabgrass?"
5. There are three things you can't be: partly pregnant, partly human or partly dead. You either are or you aren't.
6. A young married couple who find out they are pregnant for the first time don't call their parents in an excited tone of voice and say, "Guess what mom and dad, John and I are going to have a FETUS!"
7. Too many young people are practicing abstinence in moderation.

8. When I was a kid a guy said, "I knew I loved her when I saw the reflection of the moonlight in her father's shotgun."
9. The reason Planned Parenthood can't see the writing on the wall is that their back is against the wall.

ACTION

1. "I'm a man of - action, and unlike Schwarzenegger, I never had a stunt man to do my hard work."
   Al Sharpton (2004 presidential candidate) during Congressional Black Caucus Debate.
2. If you don't make waves, you'll drown.
3. Feather by feather, the goose is plucked.
4. The helping hand most people need is at the end of their own arm.
5. Influence people and get what you want using only words.
6. Those who have the privilege to know have the duty to act.
   Albert Einstein
7. We should have strangled Bolshevism in its cradle.
   Winston Churchill
8. Some problems are so complex that you have to be highly intelligent and well-informed just to be undecided about them.
   Laurence J. Peter, Canadian Educator
9. The Golden Rule is of no use unless you realize it's your move.
10. Procrastination is opportunity's natural assassin.
11. For two centuries people believed Aristotle was right when he said the heavier the option the faster it would fall to the earth. Nobody stepped forward

until 1589, 2000 years after Aristotle's death. Galileo summoned learned professors and took them to the base of the leaning Tower of Pisa. He pushed off a ten-pound and a one-pound weight. Both landed at the same time. But the power of belief in the conventional wisdom was so strong that the professors denied what they had seen.

12. The jawbone of an ass is even more dangerous today than it was in the days of Sampson.

13. Everything can have drama if it's done right. Even a pancake.

ADVERSITY

1. If common sense prevailed Columbus would have said, "Let's go home," Edison would have said, "I quit." and George Washington would have never fought at Valley Forge. But without hope and dreams life is meaningless.
2. Nothing is as exhilarating as being shot at and then missed.
   Winston Churchill
3. When an Ostrich puts its head in the sand it not only puts itself in an indefensible position it also puts itself in an irresistible position.
4. It's amazing what some small countries do in the Olympics. But then consider what our 13 colonies did to England.
5. Man was born to suffer: otherwise political campaigns would only last about three weeks.
6. The tree of liberty must be refreshed from time to time with the blood of patriots and tyrants. It is its natural manure.
   Thomas Jefferson
7. If the highest aim of a captain were to preserve the ship, he would keep it in the port forever.
   Thomas Aquinas, Theologian
8. Good pilots aren't made on clear days. Good sailors aren't made on smooth waters. It's only when you

face major adversity that God brings out the best in you.

9. Man is not made in a crisis. He's made from day to day. And what you've invested in your character on a day to day basis will determine what you do when the winds of adversity blow your way. A man's character is his fate.

10. In Hollywood what's important is fans, fame and fortune. But in real life it's faith, family and freedom.

11. Mans' greatest gift is the power of love. His greatest downfall is the love of power.

12. The strength of a nation is determined by the character and productivity of its people. Who is tampering with the soul of America?
Adam Smith, Philosopher, Economist

13. Like a boxer, if you know something you have a glove on one hand. If you are someone you have a glove on the other hand. You have to know and you have to be. That's where character comes in.

14. Colors fade, temples crumble, empires fall, but wise words endure.
Edward Thorndike, American Psychologist

15. Too many want to get to the Promised Land without going through the wilderness.

16. Everything that can be invented has been invented.
Charles Duell, Director of US Patent Office, 1899

17. Heavier than air flying machines are impossible.
Lord Kelvin, President of Royal Society, 1895

18. Who the hell wants to hear actors talk?
Harry Warner, President of Warner Brothers Pictures, Inc., 1927

19. There is no likelihood man can ever tap the power of the atom.
Robert Milliken, Nobel Prize in Physics, 1927
20. If you can find a path with no obstacles it probably doesn't lead anywhere.
Frank A Clark, lawyer, Politician
21. If you're going through hell, keep going.
Winston Churchill
22. Nothing strengthens the judgment and quickens the conscious like individual responsibility.
Elizabeth Cady Stanton, Suffragette
23. A diamond is a chunk of coal that made good under pressure.
24. Who will rise up for Me against the wicked? Who will take a stand for Me against evil doers?
Psalm 94:16
25. Our lives become purposeless the day we become silent about things that matter.
Martin Luther King Jr.
26. No arsenal, or no weapon in the arsenals of the world, is as formidable as the will and moral courage of free men and women.
Ronald Reagan
27. Minnesota - where the elite meet the sleet.
28. South Dakota - The only state that shoots its state bird.
29. The only problem with people in Minnesota taking a winter vacation in Florida is in three days you get a sunburn, come home and get a frostbite on top of your sunburn.

30. There never was a philosopher who could endure a toothache.

    William Shakespeare

31. Behold I am sending you out as sheep among wolves. You will be dragged before governors and kings for my sake. You will be hated by all for my names' sake. Do not fear those who can kill the body, but not the soul.

    Matthew 10:16

32. Learn from the mistakes of others because you can't live long enough to make them all yourself.

33. The number one Commandment in the Bible is "Fear not!" In fact, there are 365 "Fear nots" in the Bible, one for every day of the year. "I have not given you a spirit of fear but of love and power and of a sound mind."

34. We don't see the world as it is, we see it as we are.

35. God did not raise the Christians in this nation to lead the liquidation of an empire.

36. "We should never grow weary in well doing,"

    Galatians 6:9

37. All I can promise you is blood, toil, sweat and tears.

    Winston Churchill

38. Only passion, great passions, can elevate the soul to great things.

    Dennis Diderot, French Philosopher

ATHEISTS

1. The worst moment for an atheist is when he really has something to be thankful for and has nobody to thank.
2. If there wasn't a God, there wouldn't be any atheists.
3. The professor said, "There's no God, no such a thing as truth, there are no absolutes, nothing is for sure. The student responded, "Are you sure about that?" "Absolutely." Student, "Is what you just said a true statement?" "Yes." "But you just said there wasn't such a thing as truth, so what you just said was a lie." This professor has his feet planted firmly in midair.

ATTITUDE

1. The human mind is like a parachute - It's no good unless it's open.
2. Some people confuse a hole in the head with an open mind.
3. He's so narrow minded I bet he could look through a key hole with both eyes at the same time. He has only one eyebrow.
4. The mind is a terrible thing to waste.
5. Many people say they are thinking when they are just re-arranging their prejudices.
   William James, American Psychologist
6. If you can keep your mind when all those around you are losing theirs, you may be the reason.
7. It's better to light one candle than curse the electric bill.
8. What's wrong with America? Is it ignorance or apathy? "I don't know and I don't care."
9. People nowadays have to learn to take the bitter with the sour.
10. If you're an optimist nowadays it means you're simply not well informed.
11. A kind word and a kick in the pants is a lot better than just a kind word.
12. A stiff attitude is one of the phenomena of rigor mortis.

Henry S. Haskins, Stockbroker

13. I was going to buy the book, *The power of positive thinking*. But then I thought to myself, what good would that do?"

Ronnie Shakes, Comedian

14. Apathy is so prevalent maybe we should give a course in advanced shrugging.

15. Headline: RALLY AGAINST APATHY DRAWS SMALL CROWD.

16. It's time to get off our apathy.

17. Ignorance, apathy and indifference pave the road to tyranny.

18. One woman who always says something good about everything was asked, "What's good about the devil?" She said, "Well, he's persistent."

19. In spite of the cost of living it's still pretty popular.

20. We can growl, scowl, howl, and cry foul, or we can grow, glow, and go like a pro.

21. A certain amount of ignorance is necessary for a tranquil attitude.

22. One of the most expensive luxuries one can possess is to hate somebody.

Dr. E. T. Wayland

23. A cloudy day is no match for a sunny disposition.

24. Even a forced smile is better than a sincere grouch.

25. Too many people have that deadly disease called, "Bowel Optiate." That's when your bowel nerves and eye nerves get crossed and you have a crappy outlook. It's also known as optic rectitis.

26. A candle loses nothing by lighting another candle.

27. Some people light up the room whenever they leave.
28. I couldn't warm up to you if I was cremated with you.
29. Never criticize until you've walked a mile in their shoes. Then it's OK because you're a mile away and you've got their shoes.
30. The word Unruh has two U's. Which means as soon as I help you get what you want, then I can get what I want.

BAMBOOZLE

1. The Persistence of Bamboozle: One of the saddest lessons of history is this: If we've been bamboozled long enough we tend to reject any evidence of the bamboozle. We're no longer interested in finding out the truth. The bamboozle has captured us. It is simply too painful to acknowledge, even to ourselves, that we've been so credulous. So the old bamboozles tend to persist as new bamboozles rise.
2. Ignorance at the top leads to confusion below.
3. He that governs others must first be master of himself.
   Phillip Massenger, English Dramatist, 1583
4. I have never believed there was one code of morality for a public and another one for a private man.
   Thomas Jefferson, 1809
5. Those who are too smart to engage in politics are punished by being governed by those who are dumber.
   Plato, Philosopher, Writer

BANKS

1. Old bankers never die they just withdraw
2. My banker said, "I'll give you the money if you can guess which of my eyes the glass eye is." I said, "It's your left one." He said, "How did you guess so fast?" I said, "Because that one had just a hint of compassion."
3. I am getting nervous about our bank. I went to put in a deposit and the tellers gave each other the high five.
4. Our bank may be in trouble. They are giving out calendars one month at a time.
5. If money doesn't grow on trees, how come banks have so many branch offices?
6. I want my banker to be pallbearer at my funeral. He's carried me most my life, he may as well finish the job.

BEGINNING

1. The only people who start out on top are grave diggers and trapeze artists. Even the Pilgrims started on the rocks. Unless you're a proctologist; they start out on the bottom and stay there.
2. Beginnings are always hard. I heard Zsa Zsa Gabor's first husband was poor.
3. In vane do we build the city if we do not first build the man?
4. You can't arrive without making the trip, because you can't come back from where you haven't been.
5. The journey of one thousand miles begins with a broken fan belt.
6. Criminologists claim few acts of violence are committed after a hearty meal. This can also prolong the life of speakers.
   Pic Lamont
7. I've never thought my speeches were too long. I've enjoyed them all.
   Hubert Humphrey His candidacy was called, "Preparation H"
8. All work and no plagiarism make a dull speech.
9. Our speaker has all five senses plus two more: horse and common.

BEGINNING THE SPEECH

1. I'm going to try not to be like that preacher who got sick and this Obamacare nurse made a mistake and put a barometer down his throat instead of a thermometer and the reading came out windy and dry.
2. A preacher's job is to comfort the afflicted and afflict the comfortable.
3. The last MC who introduced me said, "I want you to know that Dr. Unruh is one of the best speakers in the country. Of course, if you go into the city there are a lot of them better than he is.
4. The last time I gave a monologue I was so good that half the crowd got up to go get their friends. The other half were glued to their seats. I thought it was a novel idea.
5. I want you to know that I have had the honor to speak in front of four presidents. Unfortunately, it was at Mount Rushmore.
6. I spoke at a Memorial Day service and the MC said, "First we will have Amy Johnson sing God Bless America, then Dr. Unruh will speak, and after him the firing squad. It made me kind of nervous.
7. The last MC said, "Our next speaker made a million dollars in the oil business in Texas. The speaker got up and said, "That description wasn't exactly correct.

It wasn't a million it was one hundred thousand , and it wasn't Texas it was Oklahoma, and I didn't make it, I lost it."

8. After an introduction that is way too long: I want to thank the MC for that kind introduction. But he forgot to mention that I'm also a Notary Public.

9. Ladies and gentlemen, our country is in a crisis of values. Like that Yuppie who wrecked his car and he's lying in the ditch hollering, "My BMW, My BMW!" A cop came by and said, "Never mind your BMW, you lost your left arm" and the guy looked down and shouted, "My Rolex, my Rolex!!!

10. I'm reminded of the guy who was dying and they called his son who was his only heir and he said to his son, "Son, I've left everything to you right there in the will. The boat, the yacht, the million dollars in foreign securities, the thousand acre farm, it's all yours, right there in the will." The father started fading rapidly and the son leaned over and asked, "Father is there something I can do for you?' The father, gasping for air said, "Get your foot off the oxygen hose." Well, we don't want the government to deliver blood plasma to us, we want them to get their foot off the oxygen hose so we can breathe freely.

11. I've been busier than a horse fly at a rodeo.

12. I've been so busy I've had to pay a guy to do my jogging for me.

13. With all the problems in this country, I feel like that mosquito that flew into the nudist colony. He

surveyed the situation and sad, "The opportunities here are so vast, I scarcely know where to start."

14. Tonight I'm not going to bore you with a bunch of government statistics, because research has revealed that government statistics are only accurate 68% of the time.

15. Many think that if you're optimistic you're just not well-informed. But a certain amount of ignorance is necessary for a tranquil attitude.

16. There's a fine line between keeping your chin up and sticking your neck out.

17. Don't go around saying the world owes you a living. The world was here first and it owes you nothing.
Mark Twain

18. The government has formed a new committee to study whether we are spending too much money on government studies and so far the results are inconclusive and more studies are being conducted.

19. Thank God a man can grow. He is not bound with earthward gaze, to creep along the ground. Though his beginnings be but poor and low, Thank God a man can grow.

20. I won't say I was born on the wrong side of the tracks, but we could sure hear the whistle blow.

21. An MC once introduced me prior to my monologue and said, "Tonight, Dr. Unruh will give his monologue, and after him the rest of the evening will be entertainment.

22. I almost got a standing ovation once. A guy in the front row jumped to his feet and here he was a midget and nobody else saw him.

23. When you sell your product they say you're selling yourself. That's why I got out of the manure business.

24. If a joke bombs: I thought that was a great joke, but I seem to be alone on that.

25. If a joke bombs: Would everyone please bow your heads for a moment of silence for that joke that just died.

26. One good thing about comedy, if you fail, at least you don't have a bunch of people laughing at you.

27. I learned these jokes at comedian camp. Camp MinneHAHA.

28. I have good news and bad news for you. The good news is there is no bad news. The bad news is I don't have a joke without bad news.

29. I am reminded that Socrates was a Greek philosopher who went around giving people advice. They poisoned him.

30. If the speaker doesn't boil it down, the audience has to sweat it out.

31. I realize that no speech should be longer than the smallest bladder.

32. I realize that the mind can only comprehend what the seat of the pants can endure.

33. I told our preacher that to make a sermon immortal it doesn't need to be everlasting.

34. A good speech helps in several ways. Some rise inspired and strengthened, some wake up refreshed.

35. If speaking to a very small audience: This audience must be very rich. I see most of you purchased two or three seats.

36. After a flattering introduction: After what you said, you've got me excited to hear this speech myself.

37. After a flattering introduction: "That reminds me of the guy who on judgment day climbed out of his grave and read what was on his tombstone. He said, "Either somebody is a liar or I was in the wrong hole."

38. I hope I can communicate well tonight. I had a patient who said to me, 'Doctor, I want you to tell me in plain English what's wrong with me, I don't want any of those scientific terms." I said, "You're fat and lazy." He said, "Now, use scientific terms so I can tell my wife."

39. A preacher preached on the milk of human kindness and the audience wished it was condensed.

40. I realize that all parts of the body get tired, especially the tongue.

BOOKS

1. A room without books is like a body without a soul
2. The greatest legacy I can give my children is for them to decorate their houses with book shelves.
3. Books are the quietist and most constant of friends, they are the most accessible and wisest of counselors, and the most patient of teachers.
Charles W. Elliot, American Academic

BRAINS

1. According to research only about 5% of the people think, 15% think they think, and 80% would rather die than think.
2. As long as we're going to be thinking anyway, why not think BIG?
   Donald Trump.
3. Some politicians should see a proctologist for a brain scan.
4. The brain can record 800 memories/second for 75 years. The body can get tired, but not the brain.

BUREAUCRACY

1. A bureaucracy is the nearest thing to eternal life other than the return of Jesus Christ.
   Ronald Reagan
2. We've come from *Girls Gone Wild* to government gone wild
3. We've come from Bob Hope and Johnny Cash to no hope and no cash.
4. A trillion is a one followed by twelve zeroes which describes the President and his cabinet.
5. The only thing that saves us from the bureaucracy is its inefficiency.
   Eugene McCarthy (D-MN)
6. We have the lunatics in charge of the asylum
7. Government machinery is that marvelous device that enables ten men to do the work of one.
8. The most expensive furniture in the world is the bureaus in Washington.
9. They come up with the ways and we have to come up with the means.
10. Guidelines for bureaucrats: a. when in charge, ponder b. when in trouble, delegate c. when in doubt, mumble.
11. How many pentagon workers does it take to change a light bulb? Only one but he has to be very careful because the bulb costs sixteen thousand dollars.

12. The more bureaus in Washington the more we lose our drawers.
13. The White House phones are on the blink. Call and you get a busy signal. If you told people they weren't getting a tax refund or their Social Security checks you'd take the phone off the hook too.
14. When you have ten thousand regulations you lose all respect for the law.
    Benjamin Franklin [Obamacare now has twenty eight thousand pages of regulations.]
15. Millions of laws have not replaced the Ten Commandments.
    Ronald Reagan

BUSINESS

1. Too many businessmen would sell the rope to hang themselves if they thought they could make a profit on the rope. Democrats would take the rope to hang themselves if the government paid for the rope.
   Joseph Stalin
2. I invested in revolving doors and toilet paper and got wiped out before I could turn around.
3. Job applicant: "What do you pay?" "We will pay you what you're worth". Applicant: "I can't work for that."
4. Nothing happens until somebody sells something. Salesman: "Today I got two orders: Get out and stay out."
5. I'm not an expert on computers. Remember, America, I gave you the internet and I can take it away.
   Vice President Al Gore
6. Cutting down on advertising to save money is like stopping your watch to save time.
7. If you don't believe in advertising you should advertise your business for sale.
8. Doing business without advertising is like winking at a girl in the dark. You know what you're doing, but nobody else does.
9. The business of America is business.
   Adam Smith, *The Wealth of Nations*

10. My salesman couldn't sell pickles in a maternity ward.
11. A successful executive has a wife to tell him what to do and a secretary to do it.
12. Help others get ahead. You will always stand taller with someone else on your shoulders.

Bob Moawad, Business Speaker

CANDIDATE

1. He said he'll stand on his record. He won't be able to stand on anything unless he gets his foot out of his mouth.
2. My esteem has really gone up. Now when people wave at me, they use all five fingers.
3. Holding office is kind of like dancing at the disco. No matter which way you move, you're bound to rub somebody the wrong way.
4. I never forget a face: it's two eyes, a nose and a mouth. Right?
5. He's the kind of guy who will get the country moving again. If he moved next to me, I'd move, and now millions are actually talking about moving out of the country.
6. It's useless to try to hold a person to anything he says if he's in love, drunk or running for office.
7. He approaches every subject with an open mouth.
8. He talks straight from the shoulder. Too bad his remarks don't start from higher up.
9. I trusted him so much that when he admitted he lied, I didn't believe him.
10. His greatest naval experience is when his basement flooded and his rowing machine sank.
11. His only foreign policy experience is eating at the International House of Pancakes.

12. Campaigns are so long that by the time a candidate goes to the White House he forgot what he or she promised.
13. Personally, I wouldn't want to be President, although I admit, it would look good on my resume.
14. Each candidate is accusing the other of telling half-truths. The problem is nobody knows which half.
15. Candidates tell you everything they know and then they keep on talking.
16. Believe in one thing, to err is human but it feels divine.
17. It's hard to take elections seriously when so many clowns are running for office.
18. Campaigning can be really tiring. One politician was so frazzled he kissed my hand and shook my baby.
19. The candidates in our district are such a joke the voting booths have a laugh track.
20. Politicians are misunderstood because it's not easy to talk and say nothing at the same time.
21. Gary Hart lost when his campaign song became *Your cheatin' heart.*
22. He's hot for your vote and said you get more bang for the buck.
23. I hope if we get a Republican president that he keeps his promises, and if we get a Democrat that he or she doesn't.
24. More and more Americans are experiencing the American dream because politicians are putting us to sleep.

25. He will give a bumper sticker to anyone who's undecided.
26. Challenge: How do you vote a straight ticket and keep a straight face at the same time?
27. It would be really interesting if the candidates could take a week off of campaigning to dig into the private lives of reporters.
28. His career in politics proves that sound can travel faster than light.
29. I'll sit down soon. It's difficult to bear the weight of all I know.
30. The minister and candidate Governor Huckabee said he just came down from Mount Sinai with ten campaign promises.
31. He has to first stand on the deficit and say, "Heal, Heal."
32. The first rule of politics is: never claim victory until all the contributions are in.
33. The first lesson in economics is: there's never enough resources to meet everyone's desires. The first lesson of politics is: forget about the first lesson in economics. Just promise everything possible even though you know you can't deliver. What's important is to say anything to get elected.
34. Our next speaker was born to be great. But after ten years in politics it wore off.
35. Our next speaker is rich, celebrated, accomplished, and has everything he ever dreamed of. And frankly, he has everything I ever dreamed of too.
36. Would you consider running for president? No. I'd consider walking, or strolling or being pushed or pulled but not running.

37. Greater love hath no man that he lay down his friends for his political life.
38. One fifth of all the people are against everything all the time.
39. Politicians take the money from the rich and votes from the poor promising to protect them from each other.
40. He calls his campaign promises "New Year's Resolutions." That way nobody expects him to keep them.
41. This year he resolved to be more decisive. Do you think that's a good idea?
42. If you want your family tree traced and can't afford it, just run for public office.
43. There's a new Joe Biden doll. You wind it up and then check to see if you wound it up.
44. Barbara Streisand has decided never to run for public office. That's too bad because she certainly has the right initials for the job.
45. I offered my opponent a truce. If he stops telling lies about me, I'll quit telling the truth about him.
46. "Of course, I love many things American, including the food. You know, I used to work in a Howard Johnson's restaurant."
   Hillary Clinton
47. I've campaigned now in I believe 57 states.
   Barack Obama
48. I promise to put all bills on the internet at least five days before anything is voted on.
   Barack Obama

49. I will go line by line and strike anything in the budget that is unnecessary.
Barack Obama

50. We are no longer a Christian nation. We're a Muslim nation, a Buddhist nation, a nation of atheists also.
Barack Obama

51. I believe in American exceptionalism like England believes in England's exceptionalism, like France believes in French exceptionalism.
Barack Obama

52. Who is going to find out? These women are trash. Nobody's going to believe them.
Hillary Clinton

53. California is the most progressive state in the nation. I don't think the people will have a problem with a smut peddler as governor.
Larry Flynt, Publisher, *Hustler*

54. My choice early in life was to be a piano player in a whorehouse or a politician. And to tell the truth there's hardly any difference.
Harry S Truman

55. If I lose I'm going to retire from politics, practice law and wear bright leather pants.

56. **Carolyn Mosley-Braun (D-IL)**

57. It's dangerous if you're shaking hands with a man who is bigger, stronger, has been drinking and he's voting for the other guy.
William Proxmire (D-MI)

58. Of course we're having our ups and downs. What do you expect when we elect yo-yos?

CAPITAL PUNISHMENT

1. One old lady was asked if she was for capital punishment. She hesitated and said, "Well, if it's not too severe."
2. I'm not against capital punishment because there are a lot of people in the Capitol that really need to be punished.
3. If Howard Stern would have become the governor of New York and they reinstituted the death penalty he would have lost half his listeners.
4. Liberals are against capital punishment because they need the votes from death row inmates.

CAPITALISM

1. Capitalism has spurred the greatest reduction in global poverty in world history.Almost half the world lives on under $2.00/day and half of those under $1.00/day.
2. The most valuable asset for any company in the 21st century is its knowledge workers and their productivity.
   Peter Drucker, Management Consultant
3. There weren't many ways to improve a plow until you could hook it to a tractor rather than a donkey.
4. If I had 8 hours to chop down a tree, I'd spend the first 6 hours sharpening my ax.
   Abe Lincoln
5. A good head and a good heart is a formidable combination.
   Nelson Mandela, South African Politician, Philanthropist

CENSUS

1. If you don't fill out the census they will come and get you. But how will they know where you are?
2. Why take the census? Why not just count the envelopes that Ed McMahan sends out.

CHANGING TIMES

1. It's getting so crazy that if Alice came to America she'd think she never left Wonderland.
2. It's crazy , nowadays we want smokeless restaurants, but the internet should remain pornographic.
3. Guys used to wear a dress to get out of the army.
4. A guy announced he was gay and was asked if he was seeing a Psychiatrist. He said, no but he was seeing a Lieutenant in the Navy.
5. For a long time I was a man trapped in a woman's body. Then I was born.
6. Gay wedding present: His and His towels.
7. Gays in the military - left, right, left, skip.
8. Homeless gay people have no closet to come out of.
9. How many men in a French army? About half.
10. There's a transsexual running for office. Just another example of trying to be all things to all people.
11. Will Rogers said, "I never met a man I didn't like." Now that's the official slogan of San Francisco.
12. Happiness in California is when your son marries another guy of the same faith.
13. People are getting married younger and younger. One couple was registered at "Toys R Us."
14. I can remember when the best references were calluses.

15. We used to play kick the can. Now it's kick the habit.

16. TV used to go off at midnight. At 11:55 the navy would sing "God Bless America" and then an Indian head would come on the screen and a buzzer sound would come on. We'd get up and walk across the room to shut off the TV, and there was a little light in the middle of the screen, and everyone would sit and watch it until the light went out.

17. Bath night used to be Saturday night. You didn't have a ring around the collar; you had ring around the neck.

18. During the depression hitch hikers would go either way.

19. Even the people who didn't plan to pay quit buying.

20. The Bible says, "The poor will always be with us." That's what the preacher said. When he counted the collection, he said, "they're still here."

21. We always had plenty to eat when I was a kid. I know, because if I ever wanted seconds, my dad would stop me and say, "no, you've had plenty."

22. There's a new breakfast cereal for gay champions. It's called, "Sweeties."

23. When my kid wanted a wild hairdo I said, "as your parent I have 50 percent of the vote and I'm cutting my half of your head the way I want and you can cut your half the way you want."

24. I saw a play that was so sick during intermission they served chicken soup.

25. The way the world is going I'm glad we didn't bite the bullet. We need all of them that we can.

26. Nowadays when they advertise bikinis half off they're not kidding.
27. Lady Godiva rode through the streets in Coventry on her horse without her clothes on. She rode side saddle and half the crowd was shouting, "Hurray for our side."
28. President Clinton supported curfew for young people. He said, "When I was your age I was in bed by ten and home by one.
29. When you heard a politician coming around the corner singing, "I got you babe," the bad news is it was Bill Clinton.
30. Extended families have become so common that now cemeteries are arranging for extra-large plots, so that a couple can be buried with his first wife, her second husband, his third wife, her second husband, his third wife, and her first husband, her second child by her third husband, his step son from his fourth marriage, her only daughter's only son who was once married to his second wife's first husband's daughter from his third marriage and a partridge in a pear tree.
31. One good thing about the latest rock and roll music is that when they make a mistake, nobody notices.
32. Living together without marriage is a lot like the underground economy. Doing business without a license.
33. What used to cost five dollars now costs ten dollars to repair.
34. At least we can still use a dime for a screwdriver.

35. Grass used to be something you mowed, not smoked; being "gay" was a positive personality trait, not a sexual lifestyle; "Coke" was something you got from a soda fountain, not a drug dealer; AIDS was what one did for others instead of an abbreviation for a disease.

36. Did you hear AIDS is now the most prevalent among senior citizens? They have hearing aids, digestive aids, government aids.

37. Times are getting so rough I read about a polygamist who went back to one wife.

38. Beverly Hills parents are being forced to raise their own kids.

39. Times are tough. Exxon had to lay off 25 congressmen.

CHARACTER

1. If men were angels we wouldn't need government. If angels governed men, we wouldn't need government. We're not angels and that's why we need as many checks and balances we can to muffle the corruption that is engrained with power.
James Madison, Fourth President of the United States
2. Character is what you are in the dark.

CHILDREN

1. Our kid said he was going to go to Washington and clean up the mess in this country, and my wife said, "and you can start with your room."
2. A pat on the back will give most children character. Especially if it's given often enough, hard enough and low enough.
3. It costs ten dollars per year to support a kid in India. So there's an idea for your parents.
4. Children are indeed a blessing. Without them you might be tempted to retire prematurely.
5. There was an old lady who lived in a shoe, she had so many children that her welfare check came to $149,888.
6. "Dad, do you believe two can live as cheaply as one?" Dad: "I sure do son, your mother and I live as cheaply as you do."
7. Father: "Money in the bank draws interest." Son: "I'm already interested in mine.
8. The children's lemonade stand is the microcosm of the Federal government: mother subsidizes it with lemon and sugar and dad buys the surplus.
9. Child: "I'm going to say my good night prayers. Anyone want anything?"
10. When you look at some kids you realize that some parents embarked upon the sea of matrimony without a paddle.

11. The word father comes from that Greek word *fadares*, which means "one with deep pockets."
12. Too many parents tie up their dogs and let their teenagers run loose.
13. If you can't beat them, make them feel insecure.
14. The two most important careers are entrusted to amateurs: citizenship and parenthood.
15. If one father can support five children, can five children support one father later on?
16. By the time a man realizes his father was right, he has a son who thinks he's wrong.
Laurie Baker
17. Of all the jobs I Had in my life none were tougher than the job of being a dad.
Lee Iacocca, Automobile Executive

CHOICE

1. He has the choice between two evils and chooses the one he hasn't tried yet.
2. If we don't watch out we will wind up where we are going.
3. There was a time when President Reagan was tempted to point at Sam Donaldson with the wrong finger.
4. You can never tell how rich a man is by his level of incompetence.
   O. A. Battista, Chemist, Author
5. In politics the squeaky wheel gets the grease. The mass distrusts controversy; reluctant to reconsider its convictions, superstitions, and prejudices, it rarely withdraws support from those who are guiding its destinies. Thus inertia becomes an incumbent's accomplice. So does human reluctance to admit error. Those who backed the top man insist against all evidence that they made the right choice.
6. If you're embarking on a great voyage across the ocean, you have to have some stars to steer by, and the stars have to be constant. It's no good steering by a shooting star.
   Margaret Thatcher, British Politician

7. Too many young people are going out on the stormiest sea of life with no fixed stars, no compasses, no rudders and no anchors. Then we wonder why they end up shipwrecked on the sea shore of life.

CHRISTIANITY

1. The first amendment was not written to protect the people from Christian values. It was written to protect those values from government tyranny. **Ronald Reagan**
2. Our forefathers came not to find gold, but to worship God without persecution.
3. Reason and experience have taught us that national morality cannot exist in the exclusion of religious principle.
   George Washington
4. For those who guide the people are leading them astray, and those who are guided by them are brought to confusion.
   Isaiah 9:16
5. In fact, the time is coming when anyone who kills you will think they are offering a service to God.
   John 16:2

CIVIL DISOBEDIENCE

1. Blackstone said English Common Law on human rights was based on the higher law of God and found in the Scriptures. He called this concept "ultra vires," which means "beyond the authority of man to write a law that violates God's law."
2. An unjust law is a human law that is not rooted in eternal and natural law. It is code that is out of harmony with moral law.
   Thomas Aquinas, Theologian
3. Christians have a moral obligation and duty to disobey unjust laws.
4. No law is just that does not comport with the moral laws of God.
   Martin Luther King Jr.
5. In times of moral crisis, silence is not golden, it's yellow!
6. Right is right no matter if nobody is right. Wrong is wrong no matter if everyone is wrong.
   Bishop Fulton Sheen
7. When freedom is detached from objective truth it becomes impossible to establish personal rights on a firm rational basis; and the ground is laid for society to be at the mercy of the unrestrained individuals or the oppressive totalitarianism of public authority.
   Pope John Paul II

CHURCH/STATE

1. Maybe the separation of church and state is a mistake. For instance: how do we reduce the federal deficit? God only knows!
2. This country will not be a good place for any of us to live in unless we make it a good place for all of us to live in.
   Theodore Roosevelt
3. Politics has always been associated with religion. What do you think inspired that old expression: "I was a stranger and ye took me in?"
4. The church teaches money isn't everything. The government teaches it is.
5. One of the strategies of the devil is to convince people that he doesn't exist.
6. Most politicians never come to the front of the church unless escorted by pallbearers.
7. When the President met with the Pope he asked him to help with his policies. The Pope said he didn't do miracles.
8. Liberals have taken a moral stand. They oppose morality in politics.
9. God is not dead, you just can't talk to Him in the classroom anymore.
   Ronald Reagan

10. Prayer should have never been taken out of schools. That's the only way I got through.
11. Did you know the First Amendment does not contain the words separation, church, and state?
12. The younger generation isn't sure who wrote the Ten Commandments: Was it David Letterman or God?
13. An atheist has no invisible means of support.
14. God didn't exist we wouldn't have any atheists. It begs the question because there would be nothing not to believe in.
15. We are becoming the kind of country that civilized countries send missionaries to.
16. Going to church won't make you a Christian any more than eating a doughnut will make you a cop.
17. Sign in California school: In case of an earthquake or terrorist attack, the ban on prayer will be temporarily suspended.
18. Prayer: "Lord, the money we spend on government and it's not one bit better than the government we got for one-third the money twenty years ago."
19. Three boys were in a huddle in the back of the room at school. The teacher asked, "What are you doing?" They admitted they were telling dirty jokes. The teacher said, "Thank goodness, I thought you were praying."
20. Calling Al Sharpton a reverend is like calling Jeffrey Dahmer a chef.
21. Nixon deleted 18 minutes of tape; Hillary deleted thirty thousand emails, and Nixon was called a crook.

CITIZENS

1. We, the unwilling, led by the unqualified, have been doing the unbelievable so long, with so little, we now attempt the impossible with nothing.
2. Never before have so many known so little about so much for so long. You have the feeling people are getting whiplash from looking the other way.
3. There is no underestimating the intelligence of the American public.
   H. L. Mencken, Journalist, Satirist
4. The only defense any nation can have is the character and intelligence of its people.
5. A good man will face the music even when he has to turn his back on the crowd.

CLINTONS

1. God bless the America we're trying to change.
   Hillary Clinton
2. The era of Big Government is over.
   Bill Clinton
3. People call us two for one, the Blue Light Special.
   Hillary about Bill
4. I'm not going to allow some reporters pawing over our papers. We are the president.
   Hillary Clinton
5. If the President of the United States ever lied to the American people, he should resign.
   Bill Clinton
6. It all depends on what the meaning of the word "is" is.
   Bill Clinton
7. I have to work. It takes a lot of money to support a senator.
   Bill Clinton
8. I think I'm the first black president.
   Bill Clinton
9. The motto of the Clinton presidency: "So many women and so little time."
10. His nickname was "The commander in heat."
11. People sang, "Inhale to the chief."

12. The troopers said Bill Clinton ordered all the women into the motel room. That's why the first thing he did was order one hundred thousand more troopers.
13. I went on a Clinton diet: When you break it there's no remorse.

COMEBACKS

1. When you're being kicked in the rear at least it means you're out front.
   Bishop Fulton Sheen
2. Sir, I asked for questions from the floor, not off the wall.
3. Sir, I'd probably say the same thing if I thought like you.
4. Sir, I will be happy to honor your right to remain silent
5. You'd make a great parole officer. You never let anyone finish a sentence.
6. Having you in the audience is like getting a kidney transplant from a bed wetter.
7. I'll tell you, when you put in your two cents worth, you certainly haven't overvalued it.
8. Sir you have a loud tie and a mouth to match.
9. I'm told this is what is considered a roast. Of course, they only crucify the innocent.
10. Sir, I never engage in a battle of wits with an unarmed man.

COMMITTEE

1. God so loved the world that He did not send a committee.
2. There has never been a statue erected for what a committee accomplished, but for individuals, many statues have gone up.
3. The *Mona Lisa* was not painted by a government committee.
4. Name any invention that has greatly improved mankind that was invented by a committee.
5. If Columbus had an advisory committee he'd probably still be at the dock.

COMMUNICATING

1. One anecdote is worth one thousand abstractions.
2. Liberal strategy: If you can't convince them, confuse them.
3. A great deal of intelligence can be invested in ignorance when the need for illusion is deep.
4. It's not that he's ignorant but he knows so many things that aren't so.
   Ronald Reagan
5. The difference between a liar and someone who tells the truth is the liar has to have a better memory.
   Abraham Lincoln
6. Like the little boy who said, "A lie is an abomination unto the Lord and a very present help in time of need."
7. There is a fine line between acting lawfully and testifying falsely and I realized I didn't reach that goal.
8. A snollygoster is a shrewd and unprincipled person. We have too many snollygosters in politics.
9. I will always cherish the original misconceptions I had about you.
10. He has the ability to take confusion and turn it into complex chaos.
11. When Ronald Reagan talked, people knew he wasn't lying. He wasn't that good of an actor.

12. He's a politician trying to save both his faces.
13. You should never shoot yourself in the foot especially when it's in your mouth.
14. The guys on Mount Rushmore aren't the only politicians with rocks in their heads.
15. A good diplomat must speak a number of languages, including doublespeak.
16. He speaks his mind; The problem is it limits his conversation.
17. There are two sides to every question and he takes both.
18. After Francis Scott Key wrote "The Star Spangled Banner," his wife said, "Francis, why don't you write a song people can sing sitting down?"
19. Have you noticed the expression on his face when he discusses the issues? Either his consciousness has expanded, or his jockey shorts have shrunk.
20. Nothing is more confusing than the clarification of a political statement.
21. I've learned to say "how eccentric," instead of "you darn fool."

Ambrose Bierce, American Editorialist, Journalist

22. Tact: The art of telling someone to go to hell and have them look forward to the trip.
23. An ambassador is an honest gentleman sent to lie abroad for the good of his country.

Sir Henry Wooten. English Author, Politician

24. A politician said, "I shall make a toast: Long live our senior citizens." And an old man stood up and shouted, "On what?"
25. How do you find a moderate fanatic?

26. A fanatic is a guy who triples his speed after he's lost his way.
27. The honeymoon is over when you find out there are things you can't say with flowers.
28. Any man who says he can read a woman like a book must be a mystery fan.
29. It's how you say things that make all the difference: Tell your wife she looks like a fresh breath of spring, not the end of a cold, hard winter.
30. A woman said to Yogi Berra once, "You look pretty cool today." He said, "You don't look so hot yourself."
31. I told my son to tell his girlfriend, "When I look at you time stands still." That's better than saying, "You have a face that could stop a clock."
32. A good politician gives the type of answer that makes you forget the question.
33. When a congressman is misunderstood it's usually because he's trying to speak and make sense at the same time.
34. Compromising with liberals is like trying to hold twenty-five corks under water at the same time.
35. English is a funny language: "fat chance" and "slim chance" mean the same thing.
36. There is nothing more annoying than arguing with a person who knows what he's talking about.
37. For by your words you will be justified, and by your words you will be condemned.
   Matthew 12:37
38. More hearts are won by the depth of your convictions than by the height of your logic.

39. The difference between the right words and the almost right words, is the difference between lightning and the lightning bug.
Mark Twain

40. Did you hear about the guy who was sitting on a tack? Everyone was trying to help him deal with his pain. The preachers told him it wouldn't hurt so much if he would pray and study the Bible more. The sociologists said that his pain was due to the social institutions that molded him. A psychologist said the pain was intense because his parents didn't potty train him, and he wasn't breast fed. His wife said he needed to be in touch with his feelings. Finally, a little boy said, "Mister, why don't you get off the tack?"

41. When you talk about heaven, let your face express joy. When you talk about hell, your normal expression will do.

42. A guy lost his first court battle. His friends were poking fun at him and he responded, "Yesterday, I lost my virginity, but I have no intention of becoming a prostitute."

43. What would happen if everyone followed your philosophy? Would more people be living on entitlements than putting money into the system? What happens when a vampire starts living on its own blood?

44. It is better to offend people than to put them to sleep.

45. Preach the word! Be ready in season and out of season. Convince, rebuke, exhort, with all longsuffering and teaching.
    2 Timothy 4:2
46. Speaking is theatrics, passion, convictions. . . . but it is drama or nothing.
    Robert Frost, American Poet

COMMUNISM

1. A communist is a socialist in a hurry .
2. The reason the Russians are so fast in the Olympics is they use real bullets in their starting guns.
3. Communism doesn't work.
   Fidel Castro
4. Communism maintains that making profits is a vice. I maintain that the real vice is making losses.
   Winston Churchill.
5. Capitalism is the unequal distribution of blessings. Socialism is the equal distribution of misery.
6. The goal of socialists or communists is to raise suffering to a higher level.
7. A communist likes what he doesn't have so much he doesn't want you to have it either.
8. The President wants to normalize relations with communist Cuba. They started a Ripley's cartoon TV show called, *Believe it or Else*
9. They are putting up a $20 million hotel in the heart of Moscow. It's called "Comrade Hilton."
10. In Russia. a pessimist is a person who thinks things could never get any worse. An optimist is a person who thinks it can.
11. Castro: My comrades, how is the potato crop this year? Comrades: Mr. President we could pile potatoes up to the foot of God. Castro: But we are

communists, there ain't no God. Comrades: There ain't no potatoes either.

12. A communist borrows your pot to cook your goose in.

13. Russia has many people with religious convictions: five to ten years in slave labor.

14. Sometimes trouble comes in bunches. A missionary was caught in Russia and they gave him ten years of hard labor in the Siberian salt mines. And just before he left, his doctor put him on a low-salt diet. A guy was in front of a firing squad in Russia: Any last words?" "Da, is a no good, low down, thieving, lying, enemy of the people". The sergeant turns red, stomps up to him and shakes his fist in his face and roars "Comrade, you looking for trouble?"

15. In Russia they started a "letter to the editor" column but it's a little different than in America. They publish all beefs, complaints, and criticism. But you have to give your name, address and next of kin.

16. How many communists does it take to screw in a light bulb? None, they prefer the dark.

17. In Russia they have freedom of speech. They just don't have any freedom after speech.

18. Did you know that in Russia you can literally talk your head off?

19. In Russia the airplanes are different. The restrooms are outside.

20. In America "yup" means "yes." In Russia it means, "to be intimate."

21. In Russia – no toilet paper.

22. Sign in Russian department store: IF YOU DON'T SEE WHAT YOU WANT, WANT WHAT YOU SEE.
23. Someone asked Mao what he wanted for Christmas. He said, "Taiwan."
24. One advantage to being Russian: It's impossible to lose an election bet.
25. The best way to get the government out of the red is to get the reds out of the government.
26. Communism: you got two cows, give the milk to the government and the government sells some back to you. Socialism you got two cows, give the milk to the government and the government gives a little back. Nazism: the government shoots you and takes the cows. Capitalism: you sell one cow and get a bull.
27. Rumor has it that Karl Marx's mother said, "If Karl, instead of always writing about money he ever made any, he'd have a different philosophy."
28. We'd all be so much better off if *Das Kapital* had been written by Groucho Marx instead of Karl Marx.
29. Every revolution evaporates and leaves behind only the slime of a new bureaucracy.
30. I don't get it. The Russian Republic has formed a commonwealth in a place where wealth is not common.
31. After the wall came down in Russia they tore down the statues of Lenin, Stalin, and Marx. So while communism is for the birds, it is no longer for the pigeons either.
32. If you want your father to take care of you it's paternalism; If you want your mother to take care of

you it's maternalism; If you want Uncle Sam to take care of you it's socialism; If you want the comrades to take care of you it's communism; but if you want to take care of yourself, it's called Americanism.

33. Government is like a huge elephant sitting on a tiny bird to keep it warm.

34. Liberals think that if you open your hands to dictators they will unclench their fists.

COMPROMISE

1. A compromise is often a deal when two people get what neither of them wanted.
2. Too much of the world is run on the theory that you don't need road manners if you drive a five-ton truck.
3. People are usually willing to meet each other half way but their judgment of distance varies considerably.
4. I don't like bipartisan. Whenever a fellow tells me he's bipartisan, I know he's going to vote against me.
   Harry S Truman
5. Laws too gentle are seldom obeyed; too severe are seldom executed.
   Benjamin Franklin
6. Peace won by compromise is short lived.
   Winfield Scott, US Army General

CONCEIT

1. Conceit is the weirdest of all diseases. It makes everybody sick except the person who has it.
2. He was like a cock who thought the sun had risen to hear him crow.
   George Eliot, English Novelist
3. He was intoxicated with his own eloquence
4. He is a legend in his own mind.
5. American children are twenty-seventh in education but we are the highest in self-esteem. Young people may be dumber than a fence post, but we feel good about it.
6. There are more horses' rear ends than there are horses.
7. He should swallow his pride but he doesn't like junk food.

CONGRESS

1. Everyone should watch Congress in action. It's educational, enlightening, and the best cure for the hiccups you'll ever find.
2. We've gone from "Now is the time for all good men to come to the aid of their country" to "Now is the time for all good men to come to."
3. For some reason I sleep better when Congress is in recess.
4. Reading the Congressional record is almost like a religious experience. It passes all understanding.
5. Congress has two chambers: Sodom and Gomorrah.
6. Asking Congress to stop spending is like asking the Mafia to fight crime.
7. To liberals a one percent decrease in the increase will cause the sky to fall.
8. The times we live in resulted in the biggest hope for the Republicans to be the Democrats.
9. This next year will be a year of decision. Not necessarily by anyone in congress.
10. Everything in Congress is relative. Thanks to the wimps the nerds are looking better all the time.
11. Congress is where a man gets up to speak, says nothing, nobody listens – and then everybody disagrees.

12. You can lead a man to Congress, but you can't make him think.

13. You have to admire the creativity, imagination and spunk of the speech writers of the candidates. It isn't easy when you have to continually have to compete with reality.

14. How come whenever they hammer out a budget, we're the ones who get nailed?

15. We all have to pay for our mistakes. Congress should get a volume discount.

16. He has swept so much under the rug he has to walk up hill to get to his desk.

17. My father said he felt a lot more secure when all they had to fear was fear itself.

18. Now the liberal slogan is: All we have to offer is fear itself

19. What this country needs is a man who can be right and President at the same time.

20. We have an Election Day special: turkey stuffed with baloney.

21. How many congressmen does it take to fly a kite? Three: one to hold the string, one to hold the kite down, and one to blow the wind.

22. Why does congress give all our tax money to our enemies and promote policies that weaken us? So they have someone to protect us from.

23. Why do they call it a political forum when most of us are against um?

24. It's difficult holding public office. Every so often you forget and spend some of your own money.

25. His teacher said he'd never be president. But with his attendance record he could run for Congress.
26. Maybe we should elect someone who's incapable of a sexual scandal.
27. It is inaccurate to say I hate everything. I am strongly in favor of common sense, common honesty, and common decency. This makes me forever ineligible for any public office.
28. Moral atrophy is a reward for long political service.
29. Talk about lunatics guarding the asylum: Congress voted itself a raise because they said it would make them more productive. That's the last thing we need.
30. The White House electric bills are much higher this year than last year. That's because the previous year they kept everyone in the dark.
31. The government is expanding to meet the needs of an expanding government.
32. Congress is the longest distance between two points.
33. We have too many gutless, spineless, weak kneed, milk toast, jelly fish, thumb suckers in Washington when what we need is Congress people with the four G's: Guts, Grit, Gall and Gumption.
34. Give them an inch and they think they're rulers.
35. Analysts say congressional pay raise will have a ripple effect on the taxpayer. For Congress, champagne, for the rest of us, Ripple.
36. Studies show we spend over one hundred thousand dollars per patient to maintain brain dead Americans. Why don't we just vote them out of office?

37. The trouble with the average family is that a person can't support it and the government on one income.
38. We pay farmers not to raise crops. Why can't we pay congressmen not to raise taxes?
39. Congressmen have a difficulty for every solution.
40. At one time or another everybody is motivated by a single issue, but that doesn't mean we are single issue people.
41. Our congressmen need a strong blast, to remind them that in the years past, our forefathers fled, from their homelands in dread, of the same kinds of laws they've just passed.
42. Government is not reason, it is not eloquence, it is force. Like fire, it's a dangerous servant and a fearful master.
George Washington
43. A congressman is a pig. The only way to get his snout from the trough is to wrap it sharply with a stick.
Henry Adams, American historian
44. Congressmen don't promise a rose garden but they sure can deliver the fertilizer.
45. If life was fair they'd put a tax on lying instead of gas and the government could pay off the national debt all by themselves.
46. Some call it getting re-elected. I call it returning to the scene of the crime.
47. Herbert Hoover gave his entire salary to the government. Now they are making all of us do the same.

48. Politicians should realize you can't uphold the Constitution by holding up the people.
49. This is certainly a mixed economy. We have a car in every garage, a chicken in every pot, and a wolf at every door.
50. The best thing Congress could do is go home for a couple of years.
51. This country has come to feel the same when Congress is in session as when the baby gets hold of a hammer.

Will Rogers

52. Crime doesn't pay as well as politics.
53. God heals and the government takes the fee.
54. Asking the government to solve our problems is like asking the Mafia to fight crime. We may as well put Madonna in charge of abstinence education.
55. My opponent said that money is the mother's milk of politics. You've never seen a baby who had so much squawk about where the milk comes from.
56. If no one among us has the capacity to govern himself, who then among us has the capacity to govern others?

Ronald Reagan

CONSULTANT

1. Lucifer was the world's first consultant.
2. You know what makes the Declaration of Independence such an amazing document is that it was written, re-written, edited and re-edited, debated and discussed and adopted without the aid of a single consultant.
3. The President said he may try some of Bush's ideas to stimulate the economy. That's like saying he'll try some of Clinton's ideas on chastity.
4. A consultant feels the best things in life are fees.

CONSTITUTION

1. Iraq needs a new constitution. Why don't we give them ours? It's worked for two hundred years and we're not using it any more.

2. The real reason that we can't have the Ten Commandments in a Courthouse! You cannot post, "Thou shalt not steal", "Thou shalt not commit adultery" and "Thou shall not lie" in a building full of lawyers, judges, and politicians! It creates a hostile work environment.

3. It's hard to believe our forefathers built a new nation without federal matching funds. Nowadays we can't build a city outhouse without federal matching funds.

4. We must remind ourselves that the *Declaration of Independence* calls for the pursuit of happiness. Not the delivery of it.

5. Someone should put the Constitution on the president's teleprompter.

6. You can scrutinize the Constitution and you will not find the word "fair." Milton Friedman

7. Capitalism is not a top down system. It cannot be mandated or centrally planned. It operates from the bottom up, through individuals; individuals who take risks, who often don't know any better. Individuals who venture into areas where according

to conventional wisdom they have no business going, who see vast potential where others see nothing. Failure is not a stigma or a permanent obstacle. It is a spur to learn and try again. Edison invented the light bulb on roughly his ten thousandth attempt. If we had depended on central planners to direct his experiments we would all be sitting in the dark.

CONSERVATIVES

1. There's a new book by conservatives. *Guide to Politics: Knowing Your Ass From Your Elephant.*
2. A conservative is a statesman who is enamored of existing evils, as distinguished from the liberal, who wishes to replace them with others.
   Ambrose Bierce
3. There's a new toothpaste for conservatives: Ultraright.
4. It's time for all those who believe in individualism to unite.
5. For too many conservatives their motto is: "We'll get 'em next time."
6. A truck driver taking a civil service exam was asked if he ever belonged to an organization trying to overthrow the government. He said, "Yes, I have." What is it? He said, "The Republican Party."
7. What this country needs is a ways and mean it committee.
8. In politics it's hard to spend a billion dollars and get your money's worth.
9. A conservative is a democrat who's been mugged.
10. Instead of giving the Feds the key to the city, it's time to change the locks.

11. Elections in San Francisco are different. You've got politicians with phony smiles making false promises, to voters with fake boobs and bad toupees.
12. What obstructs vision is called smog. It's called redefining the issues to liberals.
13. Liberals know how to put the suck in success.

CORRUPTION

1. Politics is a lucrative profession – If you succeed there are many rewards. If you disgrace yourself or go to jail you can always write a book.
2. Congress - these guys can create more damage than Rambo.
3. I'd like to see those savings and loan officers put in jail with their sentences compounded daily.
4. Scandal is gossip made tedious by morality.
5. It is said that power corrupts, but actually it's more true that power attracts the corruptible. The sane are usually attracted by things other than power.
6. He will double cross that bridge when he comes to it.
7. He knows how to build bridges where there are no rivers.
8. It's really a shame that 95% of the politicians give the 5% such a bad name.
9. The Senate opens with prayers and closes with investigations.
10. In the land of the blind the one-eyed man is king. In the world of the insane, normal people are considered nuts.
11. Maybe we should have a campaign obedience school for those who renege on their campaign promises.

12. Hillary looks so different in her new hairdo. The subpoena service for the Benghazi investigation hardly recognized her.
13. I heard a rumor they wanted to build a one hundred fifteen story building on the white house property. That's more stories than the Democrats have.
14. Having a coma is a lot like working for the government.
15. It's OK for politicians to put their money in a blind trust so they can't touch it. Why can't they do that with our money?
16. An Air Force General got fired for calling a womanizing, pot smoking, draft dodger a President.
17. The more the president goes on vacation the more his ratings go up.
18. The government spent a million dollars to study plant stress. Plant stress is caused by two things: dogs and vegetarians.
19. Some say he's a wolf in sheep's clothing. And some say he enjoys dressing up in other things he's not also.
20. The Clintons deny they have an enemies list. They said they have enough trouble with what their friends have done.
21. Clinton is in his sixties but has the body of a twenty year old. That is, when Hillary is not around.
22. So many Democrats are facing jail that at the Democratic National Convention they sing, "Hail, hail, the chain gang's all here."
23. We all know Bill and Hillary are co-presidents. If he is ever indicted she can pardon him.

24. It's nice to see Democrats together for other reasons than to honor a subpoena.
25. When we get piled upon one another in large cities, as in Europe, we shall become as corrupt as Europe. **Thomas Jefferson (and the reason why we need to keep the Electoral College).**
26. Every time you think my opponent has hit bottom, the next day there's a new bottom.

COURAGE

1. We're suffering with too much bone in the head and not enough in the back.
2. What we need in the Persian Gulf is a few pit bulls who can swim.
3. It's dangerous to be right when your government is wrong.
   Voltaire, French writer, historian
4. When he got married they didn't play the wedding song. They played, "Just in Time."
5. Courage is a bull fighter in a bull ring with mustard on his sword.
6. Courage is the most important characteristic, because all the others depend on it.
   Winston Churchill.
7. Skill and confidence are an unconquered army.
   George Herbert, Anglican Priest
8. To see what is right and not do it is lack of courage.
   Confucius
9. Courage is not limited to the battlefield. The real tests of courage are much quieter. They are the inner tests, like enduring pain when the room is empty or standing alone when you're misunderstood.
   Charles "Chuck" Swindoll, Pastor, Author
10. I'm more afraid of an army of one hundred sheep led by a lion, than one hundred lions led by a sheep.

COURTS

1. I know why Judge Souter never married. He couldn't say something specific like, "I do."
2. Think of all the poor souls being punished in hell for sins which we now think aren't as bad as described in the Bible.
   Frank A. Clark, Lawyer, Politician
3. The courts have ruled that being a jerk is not a crime.

CRIME

1. In Chicago, gun shops have back-to-school specials.
2. School uniforms: bullet-proof vests.
3. Three of the last four governors of Illinois are making license plates.
4. They checked postal workers for drugs and the only one they couldn't find was Speed.
5. With the cost of postage stamps they should put a picture of Jesse James on the stamp.
6. A guy saw his picture in the post office and said, "It's nice to be wanted."
7. In crime the theory is take the money and run. In politics, it's run and then take the money.
8. Immunity is given in order to get to the truth and let the guilty go free.
9. I watched ten minutes of the Godfather before I realized it wasn't the ten o'clock news.
10. I live in a rough neighborhood. I mean, when we played Hop Scotch we used real Scotch.
11. I saw a little boy sitting on the street corner smoking a cigar. I said, "Why aren't you in school"? He took a puff and said, "Hell, I'm only four."
12. I live in a rough neighborhood. I shot a deer and put it on top of my pickup and it got shot four times by stray bullets before I got home.

13. In most of the world a political statement is "Don't shoot."

14. Detective movies on TV end after the criminal is arrested and before the court turns him loose.

15. How do I look in this new mink coat? Guilty.

16. Juvenile delinquency is the result of parents trying to train their children without starting at the bottom.

17. They tell us politics is like gambling. Not true. In gambling at least you have a chance to win.

18. I put in a burglar alarm and the ACLU said I was depriving their clients of a livelihood.

19. There is no distinctively Native American criminal class except Congress.

20. A good politician is almost as unthinkable as an honest burglar.

21. A judge asked, "Why did you try to rob this bank all alone? Why didn't you get a look out man and a getaway man?" The burglar said, "Your Honor, you can't trust anyone nowadays."

22. The president's new crime bill includes a ban on all foreign made assault weapons. The theory is that the muggings won't be so bad if we can just get all those psychos to buy American.

23. A woman called the fire department and said, "There's a man trying to climb into my apartment." They said, "You don't want us, you need the police." She said, "No, I want you. I live on the third floor and he needs a ladder."

24. Thieves are just compulsive borrowers.

25. A biker walked into a bar wearing nothing but jumper cables. The bartender said, "Ok, but don't start anything."
26. Nowadays you're presumed innocent until you are proven insane.
27. My neighbor got robbed of sixty dollars.. So he went out and bought a big police dog. In six months the dog ate $792 worth of meat.
28. When a man forgets himself he starts doing things others will remember.
29. Judge: "Can you describe the guy who hit you?" "Your honor, that's what I was doing when he hit me."
30. I can read him like a book, cover up to cover up.
31. Criminals are really getting brazen. A criminal was in a department store the other day trying out nylons on his head.
32. The crime is getting so bad we don't need an electric chair. We need an electric couch.
33. In Los Angeles the high schools are so dangerous, a school newspaper has an obituary column.
34. Headline: Police run down jaywalkers.
35. The administration has quit giving chocolate candy bars to prisoners. Too many were breaking out.
36. Some brazen crook broke into the police station and stole the latrines. So far the cops have nothing to go on.

CULTURE

1. Every Tom, Dick, and Harry wants to get married.
2. One guy wanted to marry his horse – The judge said, "First I have to talk to the horse." He asked, " Do you want to marry this guy," the horse said, "NAAAAAAAY"
3. A priest was forced to marry a gay couple or lose his tax exempt status. So during the liturgy he said, "Lord I think it's amazing these two guys love each other so much they don't mind going to hell together."
4. There are too many ironies in the fire.
5. Are we a Christian nation or a condom nation?
6. Man does not live on bed alone.
7. Politics is starting to give sex a bad name.
8. We have over ten million laws, but if everyone listened to just ten we'd be a lot better off.
9. Feminists tried to put urinals in women's bathrooms but found out most women wouldn't stand for it.
10. Times are changing. When I was a kid the only bad thing on TV was the reception. That was pretty snowy.
11. Last week I went to my first X-rated Western. Even the wagons weren't covered. It's getting rough.
12. We are becoming desensitized to the reprehensible.

13. They walk around in the briefing room wearing briefs.
14. Can you imagine if the Ten Commandments had to be passed by Congress today?
15. When you go abroad on business, the best thing you can take with you to stop you from catching AIDS is your wife.
Edwina Currie, British politician
16. Art, like morality, consists of drawing the line somewhere.
G. K. Chesterton, Journalist, Novelist, Essayist
17. Ours would be a better country if people would just obey two of the Ten Commandments. Any two.
Michael Sovern, Former President, Columbia University
18. Ninety eight percent of the adults in this country are decent, hardworking Americans. It's the other lousy two percent that get all the publicity, but then – we elected them.
Lily Tomlin, Actor
19. There is no pain killer for the fleshy area at the base of the spine that occurs when the legislature is in session.
20. We may have good government when legislators can be sued for malpractice.
21. Maybe we should implement merit raises for politicians
22. Some people trace their ancestry back one thousand years but don't know where their teenagers were last night

23. The Supreme Court has ruled that nudists aren't covered by the first amendment. But they're not covered by anything.
24. What made the most pronounced impression on you when you visited the nudist colony? The reporter said, "Those cane bottom chairs."
25. Two nudists broke up. They were seeing too much of each other.
26. When it comes to Sex Ed, nowadays kids are in a dilemma. They don't know if they should pass it and please their teacher, or flunk it and please their parents.
27. People in Hollywood get married so many times, a guy went to a PTA meeting where there were four hundred parents for sixteen kids.
28. Now that prayer is forbidden in schools you have to go to a motel to read the Bible.
29. Religion is the only thing that keeps the poor from murdering the rich and that's why liberals want to get rid of religion.
30. A preacher said, "On judgment day there will be weeping and gnashing of teeth." A woman said, "But I don't have any teeth." The preacher said, "On judgment day teeth will be provided."
31. What used to be called shame and humiliation is now called publicity.

P.J. O'Rourke, Journalist, Satirist

32. I can remember the good old days when women were considered the opposite sex, not the opposition.
33. Adam blamed Eve and Eve blamed the snake and the snake didn't have a leg to stand on.

CONSERVATIVES

1. Conservatives are trying to teach abstinence and purity and morality and liberals are trying to change that.
2. Ronald Reagan never entered the oval office without his suit on. Clinton didn't wear pants half the time.
3. We live in the greatest country in the world, and I want you to help me change it.
4. The duty of a patriot is to protect his country from its government.
5. Creativity is intelligence having fun.
6. Throughout the centuries there have been men who took first steps, down new roads, armed with nothing but their own vision.
   Ayn Rand, novelist, playwright
7. Fear knocked on the door. Faith answered and nobody was there.
8. I would rather be governed by the first two thousand names in the Boston phone directory than by the graduating class of Harvard University.
   William F. Buckley, Editor, Author

DEATH

1. At the funeral of a politician, the preacher said, "What you see here is the shell. The nut has departed."
2. Over the entrance of hell there is a sign that reads: ABANDON ALL HOPE, YE WHO ENTER HERE.
   Dante, Italian Statesman, Poet

DEBT CEILING

1. Congress and the president keep raising the debt ceiling. So the question is: If you went home and found out your sewer was backed up to your ceiling, should you raise the ceiling or start pumping out crap?
2. You can't spend your way into prosperity any more than you can drink your way into sobriety. It's like standing in a bucket and trying to pull yourself up by the handle.
3. With over eighteen trillion dollars in deficit spending the question is, how do you repossess a country?
4. It's time to put the seat of government on weight watchers.
5. I love the words "revenue sharing." Isn't that what a mugger does?

DEMOCRATS

1. The communist party should sue the Democratic Party for stealing their platform.
2. What he said was a warm pile of the aftermath of a bull's breakfast.
3. Frustration is having no one to blame but yourself. So you can see why the President is getting frustrated.
4. He never opens his mouth unless he has nothing to say.
5. There are so many Democratic candidates, you'd think somebody fertilized the party.
6. He has mastered the three P's: Promises, Promises, and Promises.
7. Hearing the democrats talking about fiscal responsibility and balancing the budget would have been like Madonna double dating with Mother Teresa.
8. Here's an idea: Why don't we tie congressional salaries to the budget deficit?
9. He gave a speech to the American Indian Republican Convention and they were three of the nicest guys you ever met.
10. A Democrat took half a glass of water and said, "It's half empty." A Republican took the glass and said, "Who drank half my water?" The government takes the glass and says, "The glass is way too big."

11. The Democrats have now come up with a way to pay off the national debt with credit cards. At minimum payments of fifty dollars per month that's a good deal.
12. People can barely keep their heads above water because wood floats.
13. His idea of old fashioned values is life, liberty, and the pursuit of a fast buck.
14. Nearly sixty percent of Americans believe the world will come to an end in their lifetimes, and eighty percent of the Democrats believe it already has.

DEMOCRACY

1. A democracy is a lion and a lamb deciding what to have for dinner.
2. In a democracy people are free to choose the man who will pass the blame.
3. Democracy is the art of running the circus from the monkey cage.
4. In order to become the master the politician poses as the servant.
   Charles De Gaulle, Former French President
5. A Democracy is where everybody endeavors to live at the expense of everybody else.
   Frederic Bastia, French Economist

DEPRESSION/RECESSION

1. When your neighbor loses his job, it's a recession. When you lose your job, it's a depression.
2. Nowadays, more than ever before, it's very important how you store perishables: milk, butter, meat and money.
3. A recession is when the economy starts crumbling. A depression is when everyone realizes it.
4. Times are tough. Today we bought a dozen cans of dog food, and we don't have a dog.
5. There's a new song: "How much is that dog food in the window?"
6. I bought some sweet chariot stocks the other day and sure enough, they swung low.
7. I went to a cut rate barbershop. The manicurist doesn't cut your nails, she bites them.
8. Doctors cure poor people faster than rich people.
9. A doctor gave a guy six months to live and at the end of 6 months he couldn't pay him so he gave him another six months.
10. If they take our poverty away from us we won't have nothing.
Mark Twain
11. I see the president has declared war on poverty. Can you tell me where I go to surrender?

DESPOTISM

1. Dictators ride to and fro on tigers which they dare not dismount. And the tigers are getting hungry.
Winston Churchill

DRUGS

1. There's a new drug out that is fully approved by the IRS. It's called: Senditol.
2. If all the drugs and material medico were thrown into the ocean, it would be so much better for mankind and so much worse for the fish.
   Oliver Wendell Holmes, Supreme Court Justice
3. There's a new drug: aspirin plus chlorophyll, to help fight those stinking headaches.
4. I read about a guy who invented a drug that was so powerful you have to be in perfect health to survive the drug.
5. A study was done to determine if it's worse to be drunk and stoned at the same time. Thousands of college students volunteered for the study. The conclusion: It is worse to be stoned and drunk simultaneously.
6. There's a new senatorial cocktail. Three of those and you end up speaking from the floor.
7. They've invented a new drink called, "Urban Renewal." Just two of them and the whole landscape looks better.
8. Are we winning the war on drugs or am I hallucinating?
9. The second biggest killer in America is "Drug Reactions." I heard a drug ad which said, "If you

have pain, take this drug." Ninety percent of the ad was disclaimers and half of them were lethal. So what good is it to say, "I do feel some better, but I keep wanting to kill myself." Their philosophy is the best way to get rid of the pain is to get rid of the patient.

EARTH DAY

1. I used to be against Earth Day, but now I'm having second thoughts. Maybe it is good once a year to remind our politicians what planet we're on.
2. I used to be meek until someone told me the meek shall inherit the earth.
3. Everyone wants to save the Earth, but nobody wants to help Mom do the dishes.
4. The moon will probably be our next vacation spot for people who don't have an earthly thing to do.
5. Two monkeys were going to Mars. One said, "This is sure a lousy way to make a living." The other one said, "Yea, but it beats the cancer clinic."

ECONOMICS

1. The liberal (now the progressive, agenda is trickle-up poverty with trickle-down tyranny

2. The whole idea of liberals in government is that if enough people get together or join a big enough group they can vote for results they should have earned as individuals.

3. To liberals, a fair tax is to give everyone an equal chance at poverty.

4. The difference between a tax collector and taxidermist is a taxidermist only takes your skin.

5. Balancing the budget is like protecting your virtue. You just have to learn to say No!

6. Prosperity is getting enough credit to live beyond your means.

7. Will Rogers never met a man he didn't like? My opponent never met a tax he didn't hike.

8. God wants ten percent, the waitress wants twenty percent and the government wants fifty percent. What's wrong with his picture?

9. God doesn't pay by the week, but He does pay in the end.

10. The president brags about all the new jobs he created. The bad news is they are all in China, Mexico, or working in Washington.

11. They want to have a safety net. Well, the safety net for millions has become a hammock.
12. They want a minimum wage with a floor of which people can't go below, but the bad news they have created a ceiling of which people can't go above in the process.
13. If Robin Hood had an evil twin this guy's it.
14. The bad news is there has been no speed up of the slow down. But there is a down turn of the upturn. The Republicans are hoping for a decrease of the increase in spending but it's not likely because the democrats say the sky will fall.
15. Politicians tell us the economy is turning the corner. It's sure not on two wheels.
16. We have a seat belt economy. Everyone is strapped.
17. Headlines: Cows lose jobs as milk prices plummet.
18. If you rob Peter to pay Paul, politicians will always have the endorsement of Paul. However, the problem is we're getting all Petered out.
19. We have two forms of government, the long form and the short form. The short form the government gets the money, the long form the lawyers and CPA get the money.
20. News report. The deficit has now surpassed the money spent by every president since George Washington and it has now made the new *Guinness Book of World Records*.
21. Money talks, and the first word it says is, Goodbye.
22. By the time you have money to burn the fire has gone out.

23. If you want to teach your kids the value of a dollar nowadays you better hurry.
24. If all the economists were laid end to end, they still couldn't reach a conclusion.
25. I have a government to support and they are living beyond my means. It's just as important to treat the patient who has the disease as the disease that has the patient.
26. The fate of a nation can depend on the good or bad digestion of a prime minister.

Voltaire, French Philosopher, Writer

27. A physician gives drugs of which he knows little, to put in bodies of which he knows less, to treat conditions of which he knows nothing at all.
28. Time is the best healer, but it kills all its patients.
29. Under Obamacare, many doctors are finding themselves between the devil and the deep blue sea, and the deep blue sea looks inviting.
30. Inflation dates back to the first time a man was called upon to say a few words.
31. Most economists have what is known as *retroactive foresight*.
32. My wife asked, "What do you wear to a recession?"
33. I wanted to join an organization that fights inflation, but they raised their dues.
34. Why do they call it the economy when it costs so much?
35. A penny saved is ridiculous
36. It's a shame the recession came when times are so bad.

37. One good thing about poverty: It will stay with you when your best friends leave you.
Mark Twain

38. Patient in exam room waiting for the doctor: He saw a sign that said First call, $150. Subsequent calls $50. When the doctor finally walked in, he said, "Well, here I am again doc." The doctor checked his pulse and said, "You remember, of course, what I told you that you had the last time?" The patient said, "Oh, yes." The doctor said, "Well, you've got it again. Just do what I told you last time and pay the receptionist at the door"."

39. Does it worry you that if the United States were a business we'd be filing Chapter 11?

40. I'm writing a book about my finances. I'm up to Chapter 11.

41. The latest deficit reduction plan is like Noah hearing there's going to be a great flood and he goes out and buys a sponge.

42. You're an adult when you no longer believe in Santa, the Easter Bunny, the Tooth Fairy, and deficit reduction.

43. Things are so bad that an obscene phone call now is anyone asking for money.

44. Congressional budget hearings are a lot like Thanksgiving dinner; they know what needs to be done but nobody wants to do the carrying.

45. It's time government gets money the new-fashioned way: they earn it first.

46. One thing you have to give most people credit for is their standard of living.

47. There's a new drink: plain ice water, otherwise called "economy on the rocks."
48. They went on strike trying to get shorter hours. They thought 60 minutes was too long for an hour.
49. The economy is not too bad, this years' going out of business sale was a lot better than last years'.
50. People are cutting back. I just went to a concert by the Mormon Tabernacle duet.
51. My friend said, "I don't know how I will ever be able to repay you." What's bad is he said it right after I loaned him $5,000.
52. If income doesn't exceed outgo, your upkeep will be your downfall.
53. What's so bad about the national debt is that politicians don't know the value of other people's money.
54. The biggest problem in Washington is finding the drips that started the leaks.
55. I'd like to pay off the national debt and repossess the United States.
56. An auction is where you get something for nodding.
57. An economist knows more about money than the man who has it.
58. People who say there's a limit to everything ought to study the national debt.
59. It's hard to roll up our sleeves to fight inflation when you've lost the shirt off your back.
60. Used cars are ok for as far as they go.
61. The statue of liberty should be holding both hands up with the current economic policy.

62. The financial report was given at the ladies club: "We now have $149.50 deficit." One old lady in the back said, "I move we donate it to the Salvation Army."

63. Asking an economist a penny for his thoughts is a fair value.

64. The average taxpayer used to need relief. Now he needs necessitation.

65. The taxpayer is the only animal that can be skinned more than once.

66. The president says he turned the ailing economy around. In fact, he's turned it so much we're headed in the same direction as when he took office.

67. Why is it that whenever politicians want to jump-start the economy we're the ones who have to get out and push.

68. The White House is involved in the travel business. They have been confirming my reservations ever since they took office.

69. The most popular dish in Washington these days is Poulet a la Budget. It was inspired by those politicians who promised to balance the budget and then turned chicken.

70. Any nation that tries to make the income of the poor and the rich average is doomed to bankruptcy.

71. The best way to expand your income is to stretch your mind.

72. It used to be Government of the people, by the people, and or the people. Now it's, also, at the expense of the people.

73. Government is like a baby. An alimentary canal with a big appetite on one end and no responsibility at the other.
74. The philosophy of most politicians is: You're smart enough to make your own money, but we're much smarter on how to spend it than you are. You may spend your own money on foolish things like food, clothing and shelter. We can give aid to foreign governments with it.
75. Instead of giving politicians the keys to the Treasury, maybe it's time now to change the locks.
76. We hang the petty thieves and appoint the bigger ones to public office.
77. This bill is the legislative equivalent of Crack. It yields a short term high, but does long term damage to the system and it's too expensive.
Barney Frank, (D-MA)
78. Congress is not an ATM.
Robert C Byrd, (D-WV)
79. My definition of new money is money that's in my pocket today, that was in somebody else's pocket yesterday.
Jerry Luke LeBlanc, (D-LA)
80. I don't need a blankety blank tax cut. I've never worked a bleeping day in my life.
Joseph P. Kennedy III (D-MA)
81. Today the real problem is the future.
Richard Daley
82. One college student said, "I have all the answers to our economic problems: divide all the wealth equally." The professor said, "Well, the people

with knowledge, ambition and drive will all just get it back and the lazy bums will just lose it." The student said, "Well, we'll have to re-divide it every Saturday night. The student has what is known as, "Paralysis of the analysis" and "Constipation of the cerebrum." He is educated beyond his intelligence. He has become an intellectual derelict. He doesn't have the brains of a pin head.

83. You can't legislate the poor into freedom by legislating the wealthy out of liberty.

84. Government regulation accounts for 25 percent of all expenses. It's second only to housing.

85. Exxon had to lay off 25 congressmen

86. What a year! My stocks went from the financial pages to the comics.

87. I hired a new accountant. He's the only one who has a recovery room.

88. Our elected officials are clipping the wings of the American eagle to feather their own nests.

89. If you can count your money, you're not really a rich man.
J. Paul Getty, American Industrialist

90. You can't take it with you. I'm glad of that because my savings has gone to hell.

91. An investment in knowledge pays the best interest.
Benjamin Franklin

92. Profit is the true measure of a company's altruism.

93. From your neck down you're worth so much an hour. From your neck up, no limit.

94. Two shoe salesmen went to a remote part of Africa. After a month one wired home and said, "I'm coming home, no opportunity here, nobody wears shoes." The second wired home within the hour and said, "Send truckloads of shoes, opportunity unlimited, nobody wears shoes."

95. What you do for a living is your picture inside your frame of life. The frame around the picture is the moral foundation of America and the free enterprise system that gives you the liberty to live your dreams and provide for your family. It's time all Americans spent a certain amount of their time, money, and energy in protecting the frame, because if the frame gets destroyed, the picture goes with it.

96. The administration is trying to shove back the tide with a broom.

97. The government is failing at the job to cure poverty, but they are doing a great job at curing wealth.

98. You can scrutinize the Constitution, Declaration of Independence, and the Bill of Rights and you will not find the word FAIR.

Milton Friedman, Economist

99. The country is like the guy who jumped off the Empire State Building. Every window he went by he said, "I'm alright so far."

100. The government is now engaged in changing the meaning of words. The word *equality* always meant that all human beings were created in the image of God, the creator of the universe, which meant that no human being was more important than

anyone else. It also meant equality of opportunity. Living in freedom, it doesn't matter where you were born or to what circumstances. You could have the opportunity to learn by freely going to a library and become whatever you wanted. Today, the government is trying to convince Americans that Equality should mean Equality of Results, unrelated to effort. It is a lot easier to vote for a raise than it is to work for one. If we pass a law requiring minimum wage, we need to also pass a law requiring minimum effort.

EDUCATION

1. A recent survey revealed that there are now more TV's than bathrooms in the average house. For the first time there's scientific proof that there's more garbage coming into our homes than going out.
2. Too many young people can't add or subtract, but they can sure multiply.
3. Too many kids in our schools are like the movie, *Wizard of Oz.* They are being taught substitutes for brains, heart and courage.
4. The buzzword today is self-esteem. Self is, of course, the individual; Eh is what people say when they're not impressed with something; and steam is hot air. And so the root definition of self-esteem is People are not impressed with you as an individual if you're full of hot air.
5. Too many people have an MA, BA, PhD, but no J-O-B!
6. I find television very educational. Every time someone turns it on, I go in the other room and read a book.
Groucho Marx
7. The reason most Americans haven't read the Constitution is because it doesn't fit on a bumper sticker.
8. What this country needs is instant education.

9. It is a good thing for an uneducated man to read books on quotations.
Winston Churchill

10. To read without reflecting is like eating without digesting.

11. I wonder if any college English class has ever considered political speeches as a second language.

12. A little knowledge is a dangerous thing. That's why Washington is the most dangerous place on Earth.

13. Thermometers have degrees and you know what they do with some of them?

14. If you think all you need is a college degree for success, every college in America would be called, "Fooling U."

15. Instead of an MBA, most are hoping for an MBI - mighty big inheritance.

16. Spelling just can't be improvised. One of our senators was written up as one of the most impotent men in Congress.

17. Graduation day is traditionally held in June. The weather is hot, the hall is hot, and the cap and gowns are hot. After four years of school, it's all very symbolic. It's an introduction to sweating.

18. Dedicated ignorance gets you nowhere.

19. The less a man knows the longer it takes him to tell it.

20. Those that can, do; those that can't, teach. Those who can't teach are in charge of education.

21. Sign in California classroom: "In case of earthquake or terrorist attack, the ban on prayer will be temporarily suspended."

22. Bumper Sticker: GOD IS NOT DEAD, HE'S JUST ON FAMILY LEAVE.
23. What's that son-in-law going to be when he gets out of college? Well, as far as we can tell he'll be 65.
24. One of the most difficult parts of teaching is trying to keep a bunch of live wires grounded.
25. Zeal without knowledge is a runaway horse.
26. The only thing that is certain in life is that nothing is certain.
27. Young people think the world owes them a living. The world was here first. It doesn't owe anybody anything.
28. It's an upside down world. Government can offer million dollar proposals to teach convicts to read, while schools aren't allowed to teach right and wrong.
Charles W. "Chuck" Colson, Founder, Prison Fellowship
29. We keep ourselves so busy, fill our lives with so many diversions, stuff our heads with so much knowledge, involve ourselves with so many people and cover so much ground that we never have time to probe the fearful and wonderful world within.
30. Never get angry with a man for knowing more than you do. It's not his fault..
31. The Bible is the second most misquoted source of information in the world. The first is someone called "They."
32. It doesn't matter how much money you have. Everyone has to buy wisdom on installments.

33. The school of experience is the greatest school there is but its graduates are too old to work.
Henry Ford.

34. Experience may be the best teacher but its classroom is getting overcrowded.

35. An executive was asked, "Where did you get your good judgment?" "From my experience" he said. "Where did you get your experience?" "From my poor judgment."

36. Education is what you have left over when you subtract what you've forgotten from what you've learned.

37. Old school teachers ever die, they just grade away.

38. Obedience school is where they teach new dogs old tricks.

39. A young boy was sick in bed and his father came upstairs to entertain him. The lad said, "Dad, why did you bring that book that I didn't want to be read to out of up for?"

40. The teacher told the parent, "Your child is emotionally immature." Mother, "If you can't be immature at age 3, when can you be?"

41. A little knowledge may be a dangerous thing, but not near as dangerous as a lot of ignorance.

42. Education is expensive but ignorance still costs more.

43. A little boy was asked, "What comes after Q?" He said, "Cucumber."

44. A man begins cutting his wisdom teeth the first time he bites off more than he can chew.
Winston Churchill.

45. The difference between a wise guy and a wise man is plenty.

46. Nine tenths of wisdom consists of being wise in time.
Theodore Roosevelt.

47. If you don't read the newspapers you are uninformed. If you do read the newspapers you are misinformed.
Mark Twain

48. It is to little avail for the American people if laws are written that are so voluminous that nobody can read them, so incoherent that they can't be understood, are altered and modified before they are promulgated, and subject to interpretation so nobody can know what the law meant yesterday, what it means today or what it will mean tomorrow."
James Madison, US President, Chief Architect of the Constitution

49. To educate a man in mind and not in morals is to educate a menace to society.
Theodore Roosevelt

50. We have confused liberty with license and we are paying an awful price. We are a society poised on the brink of self-destruction.
Rev. Billy Graham, May 2, 1996

51. Tell me what's taught in the classroom and I'll tell you the politics of the next generation.
Abraham Lincoln

52. Knowledge is power, but only if you know it about the right people.

53. The greatest education for an adult is a child.

54. How did our forefathers ever procreate without one class in sex education?

55. About the slogan, "Make love, not war," Ronald Reagan said, "They don't look like they could do much of either."

56. Sign: School zone, DRIVE SLOW – DON'T KILL A CHILD. Someone wrote underneath: "Wait for a teenager."

57. Kids are a paradox. They can use a computer but not a clothes hanger.

58. My kid thought an *F* on his report card meant "Fantastic."

59. When I was a kid I went to the principal's office. He said: "I really don't care what you think of me now, I care what you will think of me in 15 years."

60. He's one of the most mischievous kids in school, and to make matters worse, he has perfect attendance.

61. Education is the progressive discovery of our own ignorance. Every day we should strive to reduce our ignorance.

62. Wisdom is supposed to come with old age, but too often old age comes all by itself.

63. If you expect to be ignorant and free you expect what never was or ever will be.
Thomas Jefferson

64. There are more wise-crackers than smart cookies.

65. The two most common things in the world are hydrogen and stupidity.

66. A great library is a diary of the human race.

67. There are two kinds of education: One is how to make a living and the other is how to live.
68. It's not what you know that counts, it's what you think of in time.

ELECTION DAY

1. Squirrels will be gathering nuts and we'll be voting for them.
2. I don't know if this means something but the last three people I told to go to hell ended up in Washington.
3. When Churchill lost his bid for a second term his wife said, "Don't worry dear, it's a blessing in disguise." He said, "If so, it is very effectively disguised."
4. The voters want a fraud they can believe in.

   During an election the air is full of speeches, and vice versa.

EMPLOYMENT

1. According to statistics there are 94 million people not working and there are plenty more if you count the people with jobs.
2. Everything must degenerate into work if anything is to happen.
   Peter Drucker
3. The only place success comes before work is in the dictionary.
4. My kid said, "Dad, I need 50 bucks." I said, "All I have is 40. " He said, "You can owe me 10." It used to be: "Give me liberty, or give me death". Now, it's just, "Give me." Or: "give me liberty, or give me meth."
5. If someone figured a way to sit on his butt and slide uphill we'd all be successful. But the rest of us have to work.
6. My kid developed a lazy eye and the disease rapidly spread to the rest of his body. He wanted to get a job for La-Z Boy trying out their chairs. I said, "If you're successful you could work for the post office."
7. The government no longer counts people who quit looking for work among the unemployed. So we could get it to zero if nobody looked for work.
8. There's an animal called a sluggard. It won't move until it has to eat. Then it moves only enough to

get to food. The Bible says, "If you don't work, you shouldn't eat."

9. "We lose two hours of life for every hour we sit. Sedentary lifestyles are obviously detrimental."
Dr. James Levine, Mayo Clinic

ENDANGERED SPECIES

1. The American eagle is no longer endangered. I wish
   we could say the same thing for what it stands for.
2. If two teenagers can do it in the back of a Volkswagen
   how come the spotted owl needs 10,000 acres?

ENERGY

1. I bought an electric car and told the salesman to charge it.
2. The goal of liberals is for the price of gas to go up to $5.00. We know it won't be laughing gas.
3. One guy finally quit trying to put 10,000 fire flies inside a light bulb. How ridiculous. I'm sure glad they finally cut off his government funding.
4. I'm sure gas prices will always be stable with the Middle East so calm and peaceful.
5. Liberals want gas prices to go to $5.00. No wonder they want the nozzle to look like a handgun.
6. At the price of energy it's not self-service. It should be news service.
7. The president wants to plant more trees in Washington. But things are shady enough over there now
8. The president has nothing in common with George Washington. He wants to plant billions of trees and Washington was famous for cutting one down.
9. Our neighbor wanted Ralph Nader to recall his golf clubs because they weren't up to par.
10. New York is paralyzed by the snow, but they are unmoved, so it's just like it was before the snow.
11. We don't have a shortage of energy, we have a surplus of government.

12. Energy in a nation is like the sap in a tree. It rises from the bottom up.
Woodrow Wilson

ENVIRONMENT

1. In my day we had pollution, but at least we could put it on our roses.
2. Our little neighbor girl walked across the road and asked me what I was doing? I said, "I'm putting manure on my strawberries." She said, "I like Cool Whip on mine."

ENVY

1. My opponent wants to exploit the politics of envy. Well, when you're green with envy you're ripe for trouble.
2. We have three classes of people: The haves, the have nots, and they have not paid for haves.
3. Isn't one of the Ten Commandments: "Thou shalt not covet your neighbor's possessions." We now are implementing public policy that violates the Ten Commandments.
4. Sign in bankruptcy court: You've just caught up with the Joneses.
5. Whatever happened to " Do not covet thy neighbor's possessions?"

EQUAL RIGHTS

1. Everyone should have equal rights, even parents.
2. Politicians may pass equal rights, but no power on earth can make it into a fact.
    Honore De Balzac, French Novelist, Playwright
3. Freedom is not the need for all to be the same, but for the right to be different.
4. Liberals believe in equality. That's why they're all average.
5. A nation that tries to make the income of the poor and the rich average is doomed to bankruptcy.
6. The worst form of inequality is to try to make unequal things equal.
    Aristotle
7. No man is good enough to govern another man without that other's consent.
    Abraham Lincoln

EUPHEMISMS

1. Redefine the meaning of words:
2. Marriage: For over 2,000 years it was one man one woman.
3. Equality: Originally meant equality of opportunity. Now it's equality of results.
4. Freedom: Individual responsibility and moral restraints. Now it's license.
5. Eskimos have 7 words for snow. Washington, DC. Has many different words for taxes. It's now investment.
6. Noah Webster's dictionary defines *euphemism* as "the substitution of a delicate or pleasing expression in place of one which is offensive or indelicate. It is carefully crafted to camouflage what is really happening. President Clinton said, "It all depends on what the definition of the word *IS* is."
7. President Clinton and Al Gore were in a restaurant. Clinton says, "I'll have a quickie." Al Gore said, "That's Quiche, President Clinton."
8. If you were a member of Jesse James' band and people asked you what you were, you wouldn't say, "Well, I'm a desperado." You'd say something like, "I work in banks." Or "I've done some railroad work."
9. In today's political economy fairness seems to have become a euphemism for redistribution of wealth.

But any true concept of fairness must recognize the necessity of a link between individual human effort and reward."
Jack F Kemp, American football player, politician

10. Instead of the word "lying" they prefer, "ethically challenged."

EVIL

1. Evil is powerless if the good are unafraid.
2. Indifference to evil is evil. Not to speak is to speak.
    Dietrich Bonhoeffer, German Pastor
3. Apathy, ignorance and indifference pave the road to tyranny.

FAMILY

1. Women know what too many men have forgotten. The ultimate economic and spiritual unit of any civilization is still the family.
   Clare Boothe Luce, Author, Politician
2. Families are like fudge. Mostly sweet but with a few nuts.
3. Nothing nowadays is fun for the whole family.
4. We went to the national convention of functional families and all three of us had a great time.
5. Man is the head of the family. Woman is the neck that turns the head.
6. If you marry a good wife, you'll live a good life; if you marry a bad one you'll become a philosopher.
   Socrates
7. If you've never been hated by your child you've never been a parent.
8. You must put up with the face, the friends, the health, and the children you have earned.

FANATIC

1. A fanatic is a person who triples his speed after he's lost his way. But the good news is they're ahead of schedule.
2. A fanatic nowadays is a person who does what he thinks the Lord would do if He knew the facts of the case.

FEAR

1. People felt a lot more secure in 1933 when all you had to fear was fear itself.
2. Today, all liberals have to offer is fear itself.
3. FEAR = False Evidence Appearing Real

FOREIGN POLICY

1. A recent poll revealed that over 90 percent of the American people were confused about our foreign policy. The bad news is the poll was taken at the State Department.
2. The problem with foreign aid is that too many countries are living beyond our means.
3. We sell military intelligence to Iraq and arms to Iran.
4. The Ayatollah Khomeini looks like a sweet old guy compared to the new head of Iran and Isis.
5. We don't negotiate with terrorists, we subsidize them.
6. Earthquakes in the Middle East: What a relief seeing rocks flying on their own for a change.
7. Saddam Hussein should have been named Saddam Who's Crazy.
8. We have a new arms agreement. Now we need a hands agreement to keep the rest of the world's hands out of our pockets.
9. America is the land of opportunity. If you don't believe it just ask the manufacturers in Japan, Hong Kong, Taiwan, and China.
10. Japan wants more foreign aid so we can afford their cars.

11. One guy turned off his Sony, jumped into his Honda and went to a Sushi bar.
12. Now they want our money stamped, "Made in Japan."
13. When NAFTA goes into full effect we can use Mexican astronauts and get the job done for $500.
14. The new trade agreement with China: They can't make any more of our computer chips and music discs and we no longer make Chung King eggrolls.
15. We cannot defend freedom abroad while deserting it at home.
16. You shall judge a man by his foes as well as by his friends.
Joseph Conrad, Author
17. Here's a toast: To the enemies of our country, may they have cob breaches, porcupine saddles, a hard trotting horse, and an eternal journey.
18. With the hydrogen bomb and nuclear age, we have learned how we can all be cremated equal. We've learned how we can all die together. We need to learn how to live together.
19. It's difficult to run an army when the General is in love with the Sergeant.
20. The Middle East is where oil is thicker than blood.
21. When you cross an Arab with a Norwegian you get YASIR You Betcha.
22. For us in Russia, Communism is a dead dog. For many people in the West, it is still a living lion.
Alexander Solzhenitsyn, Russian novelist
23. The theory of communism may be summed up in one sentence: Abolish all private property.

Karl Marx and Friedrich Engels, German Philosophers, Authors

24. To be prepared for war is one of the most effective ways to obtain peace.

George Washington

25. I move we never have more than a 3 million man army. George Washington responded "Then we need to also pass a law that no country over 3 million can ever attack us."

26. One may smile, and smile, and be a villain.

William Shakespeare

27. The last straw breaks the camel's back.

28. An oak is never felled by one stroke.

29. The principle export of the United States is money.

FREE

1. There's always free cheese in a mousetrap.
2. Along with free shekels come shackles.
3. Any time somebody got something he didn't work for someone else had to work for something *he* didn't get.
4. There's a principle in economics; You get what you pay for. That's why I tried to deduct last year's taxes as a bad investment.
5. A free ride may take you some place you don't want to go.
6. They finally outlawed pay toilets. The argument was: "When nature calls it shouldn't be collect."
7. At least at Christmas you can forget about the past with the present.
8. I've always wanted to marry money. I feel we could be very happy together.
9. The president wants to try something new: Trickle up poverty.
10. The Lord giveth and the government taketh away.
11. We are born free and taxed to death.
12. If ye love wealth better than liberty, the tranquility of servitude more than the animated contest of freedom, go from us in peace we ask not your counsel nor your arms. May your chains set lightly

upon you, may you lick the hands that feed you, and may posterity forget that ye were our countrymen.
Samuel Adams, Founding Father of the US

13. If you think health care is expensive, wait till it's free.

FUTURE

1. The future just isn't what it used to be.
2. In closing I just want to say, "This just hasn't been our century."

GIVING

1. The Lord loves a cheerful giver; but He also accepts from a grouch.
2. Do your given' while you're livin', so you're knowin' where it's goin'.
3. The billionaire Rockefeller was asked how much money it would take to make him happy. He said, "Just a little bit more."
4. What the government gives, it must first take away.
5. A multi-millionaire gave thousands to missions and someone said, "He better give, he's got it." And someone else said, "I wonder if he gives because he's got it, or he's got it because he gives?"

GOALS

1. For want of a nail the shoe was lost. For want of a shoe the horse was lost. For want of a horse, the rider was lost. For want of a rider the battle was lost. And for want of the battle, the war was lost.
2. It takes as much energy to wish as it does to plan.
3. If you fail to plan you are planning to fail.
4. Vladimir Lenin started with fourteen people. He said, I want your heart, your soul, your mind. I want you to eat, sleep and drink the cause of communism. I want you 24/7. I want total commitment. In less than fifteen years they became 4,500 people, and took over a country of 140 million.

GOVERNMENT PROGRAMS

1. We should all strive to become a government program. It's the nearest thing to eternal life on earth other than the return of Jesus Christ.
2. What is the official congressional name for meddling in the lives of all Americans? Current domestic policy.

GRATITUDE

1. Seeing gratitude and not expressing it is like wrapping a present and not giving it.
   William Arthur Ward, Scholar

GUN CONTROL

1. "What we really need is safer bullets."
   Joycelyn Elders, former US Surgeon General Under Bill Clinton
2. She believed the harder you pulled the trigger the further the bullet goes.
3. Sign: If you can read this you're in range.
4. We don't call 911.
5. The best gun control is to use both hands.
6. Bumper sticker: Keep honking, I'm reloading.
7. Don't like guns? Don't buy one.
8. Those free Obama phones have tracking devices, meaning they'll find you.
9. The beauty of the Second Amendment is that it will not be needed until they try to take it.
   Thomas Jefferson
10. If they ban guns the second American Revolution will begin.
11. This year will go down in history. For the first time a civilized nation has full gun registration. Our streets will be safer, our police more efficient, and the world will follow our lead into the future.
    Adolf Hitler, 1935
12. Peace is that brief glorious moment in history when everybody stands around reloading.

13. In a gun fight the most important rule is . . . HAVE A GUN

14. These are shooting tips from various concealed carry instructors. If you own a gun, you will appreciate these rules. If not, you should get one, learn how to use it and learn the rules:

    a. Guns have only two enemies: rust and politicians.

    b. It's always better to be judged by twelve than to be carried out by six.

    c. Cops carry guns to protect themselves, not you.

    d. Never let someone or something that threatens you get inside arm's length.

    e. Never say, "I've got a gun." If you need to use deadly force, the first sound they should hear is the safety clicking off or the hammer cocking.

    f. The average response time of a 911 call is 23 minutes; the response time of a .357 is 1,400 feet per second.

    g. The most important rule in a gun fight is always win. There is no such thing as a fair fight. Cheat if necessary. Second place doesn't count.

    h. Make your attacker advance through a wall of bullets. You may get killed with your own gun, but they'll have to beat you to death with it because it will be empty.

    i. If you're in a gun fight, 1) if you're not shooting, you should be loading; 2) If you're not loading, you should be moving; 3) If you're not moving, you're dead.

    j. In a life and death situation, do something ... It may be wrong, but do something!

k. If you carry a gun people will call you paranoid. Nonsense! If you have a gun, what do you have to be paranoid about?

l. You can say "stop" or any other word, but a large bore muzzle pointed at someone's head is pretty much a universal language, and, you won't have to press 1 for Spanish/Mexican or 2 for Chinese or 3 for Arabic.

m. Never leave an enemy behind. If you have to shoot, shoot to kill. In court, yours will be the only testimony.

n. You cannot save the planet, but you may be able to save yourself and your family.

HAPPINESS

1. The Declaration of Independence guarantees the inalienable right to life, liberty and the pursuit of happiness. So the government decided to form a committee to study what caused happiness. After months of study they discovered that well people were happier than sick people, rich people were happier than poor people, and young people seemed to be happier than old people. They spent over a million dollars to find out it's better to be young, rich and healthy than old sick and poor.
2. Liberty is not the power of doing what we like, but the right of being able to do what we ought.
   Lord Action, English Historian, Politician
3. You haven't lived until you have done something for someone who could never repay you.
   Mother Teresa
4. Life is either a daring adventure or it's nothing.
   Helen Keller
5. It only takes two to make a happy marriage. A woman and her mother.
6. The Declaration of Independence guarantees the pursuit of happiness, not that the government will provide it on a silver platter.

7. Folks are usually about as happy as they make up their minds to be."
Abraham Lincoln

8. If it is to be, it is up to me.

HEALTH CARE

1. The new emergency number for Obamacare is: 1-800-YOU-DEAD.
2. Slogan: Satisfaction or your mummy back.
3. Obamacare . . . If you have a bad cough, take a dose of laxatives; you'll be afraid to cough.
4. The new health care system has created many jobs. Every doctor is assigned a coach, and next year an assistant coach, and then an assistant to the secretary.
5. When people hear the details of Obamacare they realize as long as they have their health they don't care.
6. Obamacare has come up with new definitions. People can now die of old age about twenty years younger.
7. Undertakers are really excited. They're going to make a killing.
8. The administration took the John Bobbitt approach to health care. . . Let's just put it together and see if it works.
9. Never go to a doctor whose office plants are dead.
10. It's getting rough for doctors. Four out of five doctors can't agree on anything.
11. And thanks to Obamacare doctors are now starting to play miniature golf on Wednesday afternoons.

12. Many doctors are taking Prozac every six patients.

13. Some doctors are on the cutting edge. One said "Take two aspirin and twitter me in the morning."

14. When you add up the cost of socialized medicine it would have been cheaper to just send everybody to medical school.

15. They've now revealed that smoking is ten times worse than they originally thought, and they originally thought it would kill you.

16. HMO stands for Hand the Money Over.

17. Obamacare is like a hospital gown: You think you're covered but you're not. I don't mind a semi-private room but a semi-private gown!

18. People are finding out the coverage is like trying to cover a football field with a beach towel.

19. Business for doctors is looking up. They're flat on their backs.

20. I called an acupuncturist at 2:00 AM. He said "Take two needles and call me in the morning."

21. Headline: Three ambulances take blast victim to hospital.

22. Headline: New study over obesity looks for larger test group.

23. A hospital put in a new lunch counter and tripled their antacid sales.

24. Sign in hospital: Forget about your troubles. Wear tight shoes.

25. Ad in paper: "Learn nursing in the privacy of your home." She answered ad and they sent her a sick patient.

26. I told a patient he was sound as a dollar. He went out and committed suicide.

27. We've made great progress in health care. What used to be only an itch is now an allergy.

28. There are only three natural anesthetics: sleep, fainting, and death.
   Oliver Wendell Holmes

29. Asthma is a disease with the same symptoms as passion except asthma lasts longer.

30. The good news is you're young at heart. The bad news is your liver's shot.

31. There's a serious nurses' shortage, which means we need to hire nurses that aren't so serious.

32. Health care is the fastest growing failing business.

33. According to research one out of one of us is going to die. The question then is do you want to have a say in when that happens, or would you delegate that decision to nameless, faceless, heartless bureaucrats who decide based on global budgets.

34. I went to the doctor complaining of fatigue. I'm sick and tired of political campaigns.

35. The new definition of death has nothing to do with the heart, or lungs. It has everything to do with the brain being dead. This threatens the lives of politicians.

36. Sign in doctor's office: Keep smoking, we need the money.

37. What do you think of Medicare? I think it's just wonderful. I've had just one bottle and I already feel much better.

38. It's lonely at the top and the president has a cure for loneliness.
39. It may be lonely at the top but it isn't any thrill hanging out with the crowd at the bottom either.
40. An apple a day may keep the doctor away but a banana is more appealing.
41. A gynecologist will trace your family history as far back as your money will go.
42. The most basic question is not what is best, but who shall decide what is best?
Thomas Sowell, PhD, Economist, Author
43. To compel a man to subsidize with his taxes the propagation of ideas which he disbelieves and abhors is sinful and tyrannical.
44. We need a miracle drug that will keep a patient alive until he pays his bill.
45. Latest invention: Drive by funerals. You drive up and two windows, with a casket in each, tipped at a 45-degree angle for you to observe the bodies. Music is piped out. You sign the register and drive off. They cremate the bodies to heat the place.
46. Now Tupperware has come up with a new casket. They're much cheaper and keep you fresh longer.
47. Another guy invented a "Do it yourself" casket. You can order mahogany, birch or cedar and it has a kit telling you how to put it together plus you can use it for book shelves until the big day. The only challenge is when your friends come over it's hard to explain that velvet lining.
48. It's getting harder and harder to make a profit. Hospitals are adding pay bed pans.

49. Why did Obama cross the road? He didn't. He just promised he would.
50. Everyone gets average care. Average is the best of the lousiest and the lousiest of the best. You can drown wading across a stream that averages 2 ½ feet deep. You can have your head in the refrigerator and your feet in the oven and on average you're alright.

HELL

1. The safest road to hell is the gradual one – the gentle slope, soft underfoot, without sudden turnings, without milestones, without signposts.
   C. S. Lewis, Novelist, Broadcaster
2. I will fight tyranny until hell freezes over, and then I'll fight it on the ice.
   Winston Churchill
3. Hell is truth seen too late

HILARIOUS

1. She charges colleges $275,000 for a thirty-minute speech and tells college students that college should be FREE.
2. My opponent needs her mate because there are just too many things that can't be blamed on the government.
3. She is writing a book, *Famous People Who Have Known Me*.
4. She is known by the company she owns.
5. You couldn't warm up to her if you were cremated with her.
6. She lights up the room every time she leaves
7. Her husband's favorite song is: "If you want to keep the beer cold, keep it next to my wife's heart."
8. It got so cold in Washington they had to sleep together. She froze the waterbed. He broke his arm on the ice.
9. She has swept so much under the rug she has to walk up hill to get to her desk.
10. If she could she would steal the election returns right now.
11. She hired a psychiatrist who's deaf.
12. The less we have to do with her the less we'll be worse off.

13. She won't change her mind and won't change the subject

14. The other day she had a mental block. I think it was made of cement.

15. She passed her campaign manager at the door of her psychiatrist's office who asked, "Are you coming or going?" She said, "If I knew that I wouldn't be here."

16. She's writing a book, *How I Saved the World.*

17. The other day she said, "Of course I'm innocent, but of what?"

18. She has learned well from the defense statement: "Are you going to believe me or what you saw?"

19. He said his affairs were conducted in a moment of weakness. Just think how many more women it would have been if it had been a moment of strength.

20. When baseball season started he threw his wife out of the stands. The secret service said, "You're supposed to throw out the first pitch."

21. Do we really trust her to fight our wars? The enemy is using rockets and missiles and we would be stuck with a battle ax.

22. She doesn't file her fingernails, she just throws them away.

23. She has declared she will pick all the interns and they will be nice fellas too.

24. She declared, *Nolo contendere*, which means "Not guilty, and I won't do it again."

25. He always travels with her when he wants to be alone.

26. Someone needs to tell her defeat isn't bitter if you don't swallow it.
27. If she loses she will have to learn to drive. Her husband said, 'I won't stand in her way."
28. She took him for better or worse, but it was worse than she took him for.
29. She doesn't die her hair, it's just prematurely orange.
30. She never misses an opportunity to make people happy, even if she has to leave the room to do it.
31. At the end of the debate she was so tired she could hardly keep her mouth open.
32. In her deposition they asked her to tax her memory. She said, "Why didn't I think of that?
33. If people won't want to hear her speak, nobody's going to stop them.
34. She can compress the most words into the smallest ideas of any woman I ever met.
35. Happiness is seeing her on TV and shutting it off.
36. She said, "There are two kinds of people: those who don't know and those who don't know they don't know about her history."
37. She is like W. C. Fields who said, "I never met a kid I liked." She doesn't even love her loved ones.
38. Her motto is: If you want an audience, start a fight.
39. His motto is: A man is as young as the women he feels.
40. His slogan: So many women, so little time.
41. He is known as the commander in heat.
42. He should have been a fireman, they're in heat most of the time.

43. Excuse Number One: Really, my alibi isn't as bad as it sounds.
44. The mudpack did improve her appearance for a while but then the mud fell off.
45. She was asked why she hit her husband with a chair. She said, "Because I couldn't lift the table."
46. He carries a picture of his grandchild and a sound track of his wife.
47. She said she is free from prejudice. She hates everyone equally.
48. She is counting on people being as ignorant today as they were years ago.
49. She should never finish something she hasn't started. She hasn't started WWIII yet.
50. After hearing her I felt like the guy who had to ride home on his bike after a vasectomy.

HIPPIES

1. The hippies of the seventies, the Woodstock crowd, were the ones who said, "Trim it a little around the hips." They knew every four-letter word except *soap* and *work*. They defined freedom as license to do whatever you want. Many lived on rice in communes for a while. The problem is, most of them became professors in our universities.
2. What has three teeth and wears 149 John Deere hats? The front row in a Willie Nelson concert.

HISTORY

1. It seems the only lesson we learn from history is that we never seem to learn from history.
2. History repeats itself. That's one of the things that's wrong with history.
3. Many things that history repeats weren't worth doing in the first place.
4. If you don't learn from history you are condemned to repeat it.
   Winston Churchill
5. A nation that does not remember where it came from, cannot know what it is nor where it is going.
   Woodrow Wilson
6. Father to son: When I was your age, history was my easiest class. Son: When you were my age, nothing had happened.
7. My reading of history convinces me that most bad government results from too much government.
8. What has happened before will happen again. What has been done before will be done again. There is nothing new in the whole world.
9. We will always remember, so we may always be free.
   Ronald Reagan
10. The history of the world is that nations go from bondage to spiritual faith; from spiritual faith to tremendous courage; from courage to liberty,

from liberty to abundance; and from abundance to complacency; from complacency to apathy; and from apathy back to bondage.

11. What's wrong with the world? In two words: The Devil!

G. K. Chesterton, Author

HUMILITY

1. Humility isn't thinking less of yourself, it's thinking of yourself less.
   C. S. Lewis, Author
2. A church gave a pin for humility to the most humble man in the church. A few months later they had to take it back because he wore it on his suit to church every Sunday.

HUMOR

1. When it comes to humor just watch the government and report the facts.
2. Three famous presidential quotes: Washington – "'I cannot tell a lie. Roosevelt – "We have nothing to fear but fear itself." Clinton – "Your place or mine?"
3. You're a comedian, tell me a joke; you're a politician, tell me a lie.
4. Never lick a gift horse in the mouth, or from the other end for that matter.
5. There is no room for any liberals on Mount Rushmore because you can't put two more faces on it.
6. It's about time the meek inherit the earth, when you consider the mess the UN meek have made of it.
7. He reminds me of Joe Namath. Boy can he throw it.
8. There's no trick to being a humorist when you have the whole government working for you.
9. They said I was funny the day I was born, but the doctor still slapped me.
10. My first words were: "But seriously folks."
11. My parents gave birth to a nine pound ham.
12. I think comedians should stay out of politics, but who'd be left to run the country.

13. Somehow it seems appropriate that the most famous landmark in Washington D.C. is a gigantic shaft.
14. I had a nightmare. I went to heaven and was locked in a room with William F. Buckley and there was a podium.
15. And here's to the men in the room. May they all be what they think themselves to be?
16. If you can't pick it, pluck it, milk it, or shoot it– don't eat it. That's why in the grocery store you should shop the perimeter – that's where all the real food is.
17. A neutron walked into a bar and asked for a bourbon and said, "Charge it."
18. I bought my wife some slacks that were too small and told her to sit tight.

HYPOCRITE

1. A hypocrite complains of the sex and violence on his DVD.
2. He's so hypocritical, he's like the undertaker trying to look sad after a $20,000 funeral.
3. He has more pipedreams than an organist.
4. He's so busy learning the tricks of the trade he forgot to learn the trade.
5. He's itching for money but never scratching for it
6. We should pay politicians what they're worth but they won't work for that.
7. A hypocrite is a member of the KKK taking the day off for Martin Luther King Day.
8. The National Procrastinators Club of America still hasn't decided when it will celebrate National Be Late for Something Day, but says it will get around to it.

IDEAS

1. An idea a day keeps the bill collector away.
2. Ideas have three stages: a. You're crazy and don't waste your time. b. It's possible but not worth it. c I always thought it was a good idea.

ILLUSTRATIONS

1. A tumbleweed is an above ground plant that once it matures and dries it disengages from its root and tumbles away in the wind. If the wind blows from the east, it goes west, if it blows from the west, it goes east. The wind is in charge. In contrast, the Redwood tree grows 300 feet tall, the length of a football field. Most have scars on their trunks to reflect hard times. Some have huge caverns from wildfires. But they still grow and are full of life. They are very difficult to kill. They have no taproot. Their roots go no deeper than 6 to 12 feet. For every foot in height, the root grows three times the distance, not down, but out. If a tree is 300 feet, the roots are 900 feet intertwining with roots of other redwood trees. The roots in a grove of redwood trees are so intertwined you can't tell which roots go to which tree. Under free enterprise tens of thousands of businesses support one another to create a prosperous nation.

2. Hurricane Katrina is a great example of failed government and a breakdown of leadership. The disaster wasn't from lack of a plan. The multi-million dollar contingency plan in case of a direct hurricane hit on New Orleans was sitting on the shelf in three-ring binders. There was no lack of

resources. Relief supplies were sitting in warehouses throughout the country. A fleet of buses were sitting in a parking lot in New Orleans. The mayor did not take the lead in evacuating the city. The director of FEMA did not act decisively. Due to their lackluster attitude, thousands of people drank a drink called "The Hurricane" in the bars and streets, shrugging it off the night before. Thousands wouldn't leave because their welfare checks were due the next day.

3. A lemming is another animal who is a dangerous leader. These small rodents live in the Arctic Circle. They are famous in urban legend for following their leader in mass suicidal plunges off cliffs. The lemming leader is highly effective in moving its followers. The problem is he's moving them to a steep fall with unforgiving rocks. He has no internal moral compass, and can't manage himself before leading others. He moves in whimsical directions and others follow. The company ENRON had lemming leadership. Misguided executives took their company from blue chips to cow chips. Thousands lost their jobs and their pensions. America has had too many lemming leaders among our ranks. If the blind lead the blind, they both go in the ditch.

4. Years ago a headline in the *Chicago Tribune* said, Ice packing plant burns down." Under the caption it said, "This building had 27 tons of ice inside the building." It had more than enough water to put out the fire, but it was in unavailable form. It was *Frozen Assets*. America has all the assets and human

resources to solve our problems, but it's frozen by fear, ignorance, indifference and apathy, like the *Titanic*, which was going full speed ahead when it hit the iceberg as people were drinking and dancing, oblivious to the tragedy that awaited them.

5. A scorpion asked an eagle *if he would giv*e him a ride across the river. The eagle said, "No, you will bite me with your poison and kill me." The scorpion said, "I promise I won't. Please, I need to get across." The eagle finally agreed *and halfway* across the scorpion bit him. The eagle said, "Why did you do that? You promised and now we both are going to die." The scorpion sa*id*, 'I couldn't help it, it's in my nature." This may be a good illustration of why treaties with terrorist nations who holler "Death to America" may be a bad idea. They are shouting that slogan while they are making the agreement, and not even signing it. Winston Churchill said, "An appeaser is a person who won't oppose a man-eating crocodile in hopes he'll eat him last."

IMMIGRATION

1. America is the only country where we want to build a fence to keep people out.
2. Many young people in the US are taught that America is a racist, bigoted, greedy, slave holding country but people from 140 nations can't wait to come here.
3. Mexico's new national anthem should be, "California, Here I Come."
4. In all fairness, communists have solved one major problem we haven't. Whoever heard of illegal immigrants sneaking into Russia?
5. More aliens are moving to our country to get away from the jobs that are coming to their country.
6. Calling an illegal alien an undocumented immigrant is like calling a drug dealer an unlicensed pharmacist.
7. Never brag about your grandparents coming over on the Mayflower. The immigration laws weren't as strict in those days.
8. When you see the other side chopping off heads, water boarding doesn't sound so severe.
   Donald Trump
9. Illegal Immigrants are flooding the US. Proposal: Put the guy who found the two contaminated grapes and thereby destroyed a billion dollars' worth of Chilean fruit, in charge of immigration.

10. I swear if immigrants coming across the border from Mexico were evangelical Christians hoping to home school their kids, the president would call out the Marines and National Guard.

INSULTS

1. I'm trying to see things from your point of view but I can't get my head up my rear end that far.
2. There is only one cure for your gray hair and it was invented by a Frenchman. It's called the guillotine.
3. If everyone knew what each said of the other, there would not be four friends in the world.
   Blaise Pascal, French Mathematician, Writer
4. There is no evidence that his tongue is connected to his brain.
5. You can't act like a skunk without people getting wind of it.
6. Inviting a liberal to the party is like inviting a pyromaniac to a housewarming party.
7. Light travels faster than sound. That's why my opponent appears bright until he speaks.
8. He's an expert at playing the game of telling us how to get out of the trouble the government got us into.
9. The president spends half his time making promises and the other half making excuses.
10. He has mastered the art of double speak.
11. He should have a clean mind because he changes it so often.
12. In fact, he changes sides more often than a windshield wiper.

13. He calls it brainstorming but it was really more like a light drizzle.
14. There's no fool like an old fool. You just can't beat all that experience.
15. I have a scientific word to describe his philosophy, and the word is NUTS!
16. How could such a big head have such a little mind?
17. He's a man of convictions - in fact he's had ten of them.
18. He's the kind of guy who can walk into an empty room and blend right in.
19. She has the personality that is a cross between a pothole, a speed bump, and a dial tone.
20. I'll accept your opinion for what it's worth. You owe me $10.
21. The less you see her, the better you like her.
22. She loves to shoot from the lip.
23. I'd love to give her my new invention: A boomerang attached to a hand grenade.
24. A sharp nose indicates curiosity. A flat nose indicates too much curiosity.
25. I've had cases of love that were only infatuation, but this hatred I feel for you is the real thing.
26. Sir, your mouth is so big I bet you could eat a banana sideways.
27. He's a legend in his own mind.
28. This is a time for turkeys. Farmers are raising them, butchers are selling them, and democrats are running them.
29. What he needs is a set of Velcro lips.

30. Would you buy a used snow blower from my opponent?
31. The president went to his high school reunion and they took back his "Most likely to succeed" award.
32. The fine line between sanity and madness has just gotten finer.
33. To him virtue is insufficient temptation.
34. He can resist anything but temptation.
35. He had every attribute of a dog except loyalty.
36. He said he'd rather be right than president. Don't worry, you'll never be either.
37. He can do the work of two men: Laurel and Hardy.

INNOVATION

1. Businesses now have to innovate to succeed: My undertaker added a gift shop onto his mortuary. His motto is shop till you drop.
2. My veterinarian added a taxidermy shop on to his. His motto is either way you get your dog back.
3. Our diet center built a doughnut shop next door to get them coming and going.
4. Need to make pencils with an eraser at both ends for people who can't do anything right.
5. Whoever invented bungee jumping must have watched a lot of Road Runner cartoons.
6. I'll try anything once. Even Limburger cheese.
   Albert Einstein
7. My wife invented a new cologne for me. It's called "Old Spouse."
8. So I decided to give her some "Oil of Old Lady."
9. High heels was invented by a girl who got kissed on the forehead.
10. When you cross McDonald's with Apple Computer you get a Big McIntosh.
11. The secret is to never let your good fortune nor your bad fortune spoil you.
12. One music historian observed that Bach did most of his composing while lying in bed after a nap. He also had 19 children.

13. Having things drilled into you can be boring.
14. My fortune cookie the other day said, "For a refreshing change of pace try McDonalds."

INTELLECTUALS

1. There are some things only intellectuals are crazy enough to believe.
2. They have spent a great deal of time shoveling smoke.
3. You want to have a battle of wits. I'll check my brains and we'll be even.

JURY

1. Twelve people of average ignorance
2. I got married by a judge, but I should have had a jury.
3. Jury inquiry question: "Sir, do you have any reason to be prejudiced in this case?" Juror: "Yes I do. I just took one look at that guy and I knew he was guilty as sin." Lawyer: "Sir, you're pointing at the prosecuting attorney."

JUSTICE

1. In America it seems, nobody wants justice.
2. Reason and experience have taught us that national morality cannot exist in the exclusion of religious principle.
    George Washington
3. We have the choice now between preserving our Christian heritage and principles or reverting back to Barbaric Paganism.
    Theodore Roosevelt

LAWYERS

1. A high priced lawyer, low priced lawyer, and the tooth fairy were sitting around a table that had 100 dollar bill on it. Suddenly the lights went out and came back on and the bill was gone. Who took it? Obviously, it was the high priced lawyer, because the low priced lawyer and tooth fairy are just figments of your imagination.

2. Imagine the appeals, dissents and remandments, if lawyers had written the Ten Commandments.
   Harry J. Bender

3. When God gave Moses the Ten Commandments he said, "You realize Lord that this may lead to the creation of lawyers!"

4. Lawyers know where there's a will, there's a way to break it.
   Ruth K. Burke, Attorney

5. A man told his lawyer he embezzled $150,000 in the safety deposit box. He said, "They have a pretty good case against me. Do you think I have a chance? The lawyer said, "I guarantee you that you'll never go to prison with all that money." He didn't. He went to jail flat broke.

6. He passed the bar years ago and hasn't passed one since.

7. My lawyer is so bad, if I ever have to plead insanity, he will be exhibit A

8. Three Philadelphia lawyers are no match for the devil.

9. The lawyer's prayer: "Lord, stir up strife among thy people, lest thy servant hunger."

10. Hell hath no fury like the lawyer of a woman scorned.

LEADERSHIP

1. I must follow the people, I'm their leader.
   Benjamin Disraeli, former UK Prime Minister
2. Liberals - I believe in benevolent dictatorship provided I am the dictator.
   Richard Branson, Founder of Virgin Group
3. George Washington was our first president. Before that Americans only had themselves to blame.
4. George Washington never told a lie. He could never get elected today.
5. It is hard to look up to a leader who keeps his ear to the ground.
   James H. Boren, Humorist
6. The final test of a leader is that he leaves behind the will and convictions to carry on.
   Walter Lippmann, Author, Reporter
7. Leaders always choose the harder rather than the easy wrong.
8. Solomon, the wisest man of all time, said, "Consider the ant, observe her ways and be wise. The ant drives itself even though it has no commander. It needs no constant cheerleading to gather food. It leads and manages itself.
9. The first responsibility of a leader is to define reality. The last is to say "thank you." In between the two the leader must become a servant and a debtor.
   Max De Pree, Business Author

LIBERALS

1. When liberals got elected it was the dawn of a new error.
2. He wants to run again and he'll probably win. Sure, they always return to the scene of the crime.
3. Democratic headquarters should have mistletoe over their door so people can kiss their money goodbye when they are elected.
4. I think my dog's a Democrat. I'm just basing it on what he does every time he sees a bush.
5. He can't get over being labeled with the "L" word. Loser.
6. Liberals are trying to solve the nation's garbage problem. Unfortunately, most don't know a landfill from a hole in the ground.
7. Sometimes a cigar is just a cigar.
   Sigmund Freud
8. Personally, I don't like liberal jokes. Too many get elected.
9. I saw a tombstone: "Here lies a liberal and a good man." I didn't know you could bury two people in one grave.
10. Under Obamacare, a liberal having his conscience removed is a minor operation.
11. Liberals can understand everything except people who don't understand them.

12. A liberal has his feet planted firmly in midair.

13. Opponents argue that a conservative Supreme Court could take us back to the days when criminals were considered second-class citizens.

14. The difference between a vulture and a liberal is a vulture at least waits until you're dead before he eats your heart out.

15. A liberal will give you the shirt off my back.

16. A liberal gave his wife an X-ray of his chest. He said, "Honey, I couldn't give you anything but I want you to know my heart's in the right place."

17. He promised to help all the poor people. If you vote for him we'll all be poor.

18. Tonight, watch Evel Knievel jump over twenty liberals with a steam roller.

19. A lecherous politician drools out of both sides of his mouth at the same time.

20. Liberals have the best relay teams. They're always passing the buck.

21. Every reform movement has a lunatic fringe.

22. In the light of subsequent events, whatever we do now will probably seem ironic, tragic, or silly.

23. Liberals are passing the buck but they're hanging onto the tens and twenties.

24. God helps those who help themselves; and liberals, those who don't.

25. How many liberals does it take to screw in a light bulb? One to screw it in and the rest to vote the power company a rate hike.

26. How many liberals does it take to screw in a light bulb? One. They hold onto the socket and wait for the world to revolve around them.

27. How many liberals does it take to screw in a light bulb? None, they prefer the dark.

28. Liberal astronomer: "Man is nothing but an infinitesimal dot in an infinitesimal universe." The philosopher said, "Yes, but that infinitesimal dot is still an astronomer."

29. We must preserve retirement income, we must preserve Medicare, and we must preserve Social Security. Liberals are the party of the well-preserved.

30. Republicans believe charity begins in the home. Liberals believe it begins in the House.

31. Liberals don't spend money like drunken sailors because drunken sailors spend their own money.
Ronald Reagan

32. Two can live as cheaply as one, but only half as long.

33. We're all in this alone.

34. It's time to put the "Od" in charge of the "Id."

35. Faith is believing what you know ain't so.
Mark Twain

36. Too many liberal women are pure as the driven slush.

37. The goal of liberals is not to make things better, but to make things worse slower.

38. How do you know if a liberal is dead? His heart stops bleeding.

39. What's the difference between baseball and politics? In baseball if you're caught stealing you're out.

40. When baiting a mousetrap with cheese, always leave enough room for the mouse.
41. I put egg on my face at a costume party and went as a liberal economist.

Ronald Reagan

42. It's better to be approximately right than precisely wrong.
43. Liberals depend on your ignorance and confidence. When they tell you Obamacare is an opportunity of a life time you need to ask if it's your life time or theirs?
44. The more liberals are in error the more they think they're right.
45. People are starting to take comedians seriously and politicians as a joke.
46. Up until now, Herbert Hoover was the only president who ever had a depression named after him.
47. Obama is so narcissistic, he will try to re-write the history of the world in one volume and his biography in two.
48. I wish politicians would start thinking inside the box.
49. Statistics have revealed that 99 out of 100 liberal ideas that come down the road lead to a dead end.
50. Liberal philosophy: There is no problem so difficult that it can't be solved by brute force and taking advantage of people's ignorance.
51. Politicians are trying to lecture us on navigation while the ship of state is sinking.

LIBERAL LUNACY

1. Dennis Rodman wanted to change his name to "orgasm" That's because "dumb schmuck" was already taken.
2. Re: Obamacare: We have to pass it so we can find out what's in it.
   Nancy Pelosi (D-CA)
3. Why would I read it? I'd have to hire a team of lawyers to explain it to me and what good would that do?
   John Cornyn (R-TX)
4. Don't ask us to read this thing. That would be cruel and unusual punishment.
   US Supreme Court regarding Obamacare
5. The question is whether changing the deck chairs on the *Titanic* is the way to go.
   Ted Kennedy (D-MA)
6. I was never a bad person. I made some mistakes. I just needed to mature.
   Monica Lewinski, former Clinton White House intern
7. In the sixties a book was written: "Revolution for the Hell of it." The beatniks said "If we overthrow the government where are we going to get our welfare checks?"

LIBERAL SLOGANS

1. If at first you don't succeed, lie, lie again.
2. If you can't convince 'em, confuse' em.
3. How can we fool 'em today?
4. You can fool some of the people all of the time, and all of the people some of the time, and apparently that's enough.
5. So many women and so little time.
6. You can lead a horse to water but can't make him drink; you can send a liberal to Washington but you can't make him think.
7. He said the whole world was a string, but he's just stringing us along.
8. There's no problem so big it can't be covered up.
9. We have nothing to offer but fear itself.
10. I regret that I have but one wife to give for my country.
11. Liberal song: "Inhale to the chief."
12. He's known as the commander in heat.
13. Also known as the commander in briefs.
14. It's given new meaning to the word "debriefing."
15. He needs to learn the meaning of the word "IS, because he has proven the government IS not the solution, it IS the problem!
16. The important thing is sincerity. If you can fake that you've got it made.

17. Hope and change has turned into hype and chains.
18. If you can't take the heat, stay out of the hot tub.
19. It's much easier to be feared than loved.
20. Win one for the zipper.
21. Never believe anything until it's been officially denied.
22. Lord, help me be pure; but not yet.
23. An evil mind is a constant solace.
24. A thing worth having is worth cheating for.
   W. C. Fields
25. My only a version to vice is the price.
   Victor Buono, American Actor, Comic
26. Tax to the max, spend to the end.
27. Liberals would make great bank tellers, because they can't keep their hands off other people's money.
28. Liberals always guarantee that the cream will always rise to the middle.

LIBERTY

1. Patrick Henry's wife said, "Patrick, I know how you feel about liberty, but this is your third night out this week!"
2. James Madison said, "If we let people govern themselves, they could rape, rob and murder each other." John Adams responded, "Yes, freedom without virtue is madness." Freedom and self-government require two things: virtue and individual responsibility. Without them there is no freedom. As late as 1776, 98 percent of the people believed in the God of the Bible. They concluded it was worth the experiment to allow the power to be in the hands of the people. But they also understood man's sinful nature. Power corrupts. That's why they put in as many checks and balances as they could to hold each other accountable. John Adams said, "The Constitution was written for moral people, it is woefully inadequate for the government of any other." George Washington said, "It is impossible to govern without God and the Bible."
3. Liberty means responsibility. That's why most men dread it.
4. At an early age I discovered I was not God.
5. The best way to demonstrate a crooked stick is to lay a straight one beside it.

6. The steamship *Titanic* struck an iceberg and sank on April 15, 1912. One favorite fact about the tragedy is that the ship went down in less time than it took to watch the movie of the same name.

LIFE

1. Everything has been figured out except how to live.
2. There is more to life than increasing its speed.
Mahatma Gandhi
3. As lousy as things are now, tomorrow they will be somebody's good old days.
Gerald Barzan, Humorist
4. When you have an elephant by the hind leg and he's running away, it's best to let him go.
Abraham Lincoln
5. Adults always ask kids what they're going to be when they grow up because they're looking for ideas.
6. People waste more time waiting for someone to take charge of their lives than they do in any other pursuit.
7. Most happiness is lost in the pursuit of it.
8. I could dance with you till the cows come home. On second thought, I'd rather dance with the cows till you come home.
Groucho Marx
9. Thousands of years ago man discovered fire, and he's been playing with it ever since.
10. If you only get out of life what you put into it, how are you supposed to keep up with inflation?
11. Far and away the best that life offers is a chance to work hard at work worth doing.
Theodore Roosevelt

12. Some of the world's most disappointed people are the ones who get what's coming to them.

13. A pessimist stays seasick during the entire voyage of life.

14. If you don't watch out you are going to end up where you are going.

15. The test of a fulfilling life is what we are willing to settle for.

16. Leisure is the mother of philosophy.

17. Life is like an onion:. You peel it away one layer at a time, and sometimes you weep.

18. Life insurance keeps a man poor so he can die rich.

19. A guy was 97 and said he didn't have an enemy in the world. The last one passed away last year.

20. My junk mail is starting to come postage due.

21. He who hesitates is often wise.

22. People looking at a guy in a casket saying, "Look how peaceful he looks, how relaxed, so tan, so healthy." "Why not"? Replied Middleman, "He just spent three weeks in Miami."

23. Did you ever get the feeling you're surrounded by incompetents and it's beginning to rub off?
   Lewis Stoltz

24. I used to be up a creek without a paddle; now I'm down the information highway without a modem.

25. Experience is a hard teacher because she gives the test first and the lesson afterwards.
   Vernon Sanders Law, Pitcher, Pittsburgh Pirates

26. Aloneness is not loneliness. If you can't enjoy your own company, you can't expect others to.

27. You will never be the person you can be if pressure, tension, and discipline are taken out of your life.

28. Sometimes a first impression is a permanent dent.

29. When you're bogged down with trouble you discover who your friends are. They're the ones that got you into this mess.

30. You can't take it with you. One guy said, "I'm glad of that because my savings have gone to hell."

31. Man blames fate for other people's accidents, but he feels personally responsible when he gets a hole in one.

32. Sometimes when they say you're ahead of your time, what they really mean is you have a lousy sense of timing.

33. If truth were beauty, how come nobody has their hair done in a library?

34. Assumption is the mother of screw ups.
Eugene Lewis Fordsworth

35. Where is the life we have lost in living? Where is the wisdom we have lost in knowledge? Where is the knowledge we have lost in information? We have knowledge of motion but not stillness (Be still and know that I am God.) Knowledge of speech but not silence (in solitude we venture into the depth of thinking.) Knowledge of words, but not THE WORD.

36. There is the greatest practical benefit in making a few failures early in life.
Thomas Henry Huxley, British Biologist

37. Never retire. Do what you do and keep doing it. Live fully and never retreat; that is, unless you're lifting potatoes.

38. I'm at the age when I'm starting to see things as they really are.

39. There are two ways to live your life. One as if nothing is a miracle and the other as if everything is a miracle.
Albert Einstein

40. The good old days back then were called "These trying times."

41. I'm an old man and have known many troubles. Most of them never happened.
Mark Twain

42. It's good to do or say at least one outrageous thing a week.

43. Life is not a beauty contest.

44. Maturity is deciding which bridges to cross and which to burn.

45. I want to die young at an advanced age.

46. Seeing life as sacred is costly. It could cost you your envy, pride, malice and anger; a price too many liberals are unwilling to pay.

47. There is nothing so bad it can't masquerade as moral. Hitler called his a Liberation Army.

48. This country is coming to the bridge we said we'd cross when we came to it.

49. Whenever you find you are on the side of the majority, it's time to pause and reflect.

50. The future, though imminent, is obscure.
(Attributed to Winston Churchill)

51. To error is human but the eraser of government has worn out before the pencil.

LOBBYISTS

1. A lobbyist is a guy who, when push comes to shove, depends on pull.
2. How many lobbyists does it take to screw in a light bulb? None; but by offering an all-expense paid trip to the Bahamas they can get a congressman to do it.

LOVE

1. A bell's not a bell till you ring it, a song's not a song till you sing it, and love in your heart is not put there to stay, love isn't love, till you give it away.
2. Love is the most talked about, written about, sung about, and read about subject in the world, but the paradox is: It is the least understood.
3. My wife said she knew I loved her because when I look at her it's the same look as when I look in the refrigerator.
4. Love is listening when another is speaking, overlooking petty faults and forgiving all failure, valuing other people for who they are, and expressing love in your own way.

MARIJUANA

1. When I was a kid pot was something you put under the bed so you didn't have to take the trip.
2. We've come from a chicken in every pot to being a country run by a bunch of pot smoking chickens.
3. Pot isn't habit forming. I know because I haven't inhaled it for years.
   Bill Clinton
4. A lot of people are under the influence of dope. On Election Day we find out which ones.
5. There is a big difference between thinking you're more creative on dope and actually being more creative. You can get high and think you can whip Joe Frazier in the ring, but doing so is another story.
6. It's not hard to quit smoking. I've quit a thousand times.
   Mark Twain
7. My father taught me that Marijuana would cause brain damage, because if he caught me doing it he was going to break my head.

MEDIA

1. I never miss your column. Never read it so I never miss it.
2. I just figured out why newsmen are called anchors. When they want to get to the bottom of something, they always go overboard and sink pretty low.
3. Freedom of the press is limited to those who own one.
4. The news is often more distorted than reported, more tinted than printed.

MEETINGS

1. We'd like to get this meeting started. Would you all please take your seats and put them in the nearest chair?
2. Meetings: They waste hours but keep the minutes.

MEMORY

1. I can remember what people said but I can't always remember who said them. For instance, I can't remember if it was Will Rogers or Liz Taylor who said, "I never met a man I didn't like."
2. I can remember the day I was born. I was so shocked I couldn't talk for two years.
3. Doctor to patient: "What's your problem?" Patient: "I lost my memory." Doctor: "How long have you had this problem?" Patient: "What problem?"

MIDDLE OF THE ROAD

1. Democrats say they are in the middle of the road. So are the potholes.
2. The middle of the road is the most dangerous place; you get hit from both sides
3. That's also where dead raccoons and possums are.
4. Too many people want to be in the front of the bus, the back of the church and the middle of the road.

MINIMUM WAGE

1. The minimum wage has gone up. Now, if we could just do something about minimum effort.

2. A gal wanted me to sign a petition to put minimum wage on the ballot. I asked her, "Are you getting paid to hand out this petition?" She said, "Yes." I asked, "How much?" She said, "Minimum wage." I asked, "If you think you're worth $10 per hour, why you are willing to work for $7.50? And why are the people telling you that you're worth $10 per hour not paying you a dime more than $7.50? Isn't that the ultimate in hypocrisy?" So I asked, "If I ran a restaurant and couldn't afford to pay you minimum wage how much would you be making?" She said, "Nothing." So I asked, "If you had no money would you rather make $7.50 per hour or nothing? It's called "FREE ENTERPRISE." I said, "I guess it's a lot easier to vote for a raise than it is to earn it, isn't it?"

MONEY

1. Follow the money. A fool and his money are soon courted.
2. An honest politician is one who when he's bought, stays bought.
3. An honest politician is one who doesn't steal on Sundays.
4. Don't steal, the government hates the competition.
5. The poor will always be with you.
   Matthew 26:11
6. Thief with gun to a guy's head in Washington: "Give me your money." Man: "You can't rob me." Thief: "Why not?" Because I'm a US Senator." The thief said, "OK, give me MY MONEY!"
7. The last time there was teamwork in Washington was when Congress voted itself a raise.
8. Women prefer men who have something tender about them - especially the legal kind.
   Kay Ingram, British Investor
9. We're always broke. We save money for a rainy day. We live in Seattle.
10. Money can't buy happiness. They've proven that a man with $10 million is no happier than a man with $9 million.
11. If a rich guy has funny ways he's considered "eccentric." If a poor guy has funny ways he's considered "NUTS!"

12. The bulls and bears are not as bad as the bum steers.
13. My grandfather came to this country and only spoke three words of English and became a multi-millionaire in three months. What were those three words? Stick' em up.
14. Some think Washington is the home of the funding fathers.
15. People are either on welfare, unemployment or sedatives.
16. The only people who have ends meet are in a crowded bus.
17. I was asked, "What is your new book about?" I said about $29.95.
18. A fool and his money are soon parted. That phrase was coined before federal bailouts.
19. How did a fool and his money get together in the first place?
20. Virtue has never been as respectable as money.
   Mark Twain
21. Nothing succeeds like the appearance of success.
22. The average person can no longer afford prosperity. Congress has lost the war on poverty, but they sure are trying hard to cure success.
23. A billion dollars would take 1,143 one-ton trucks to take to the bank.
24. I wouldn't mind going to Washington someday just to be near my money.
25. There was a time when a fool and his money were soon parted. With the liberals in power, it now happens to everyone.
26. The love of someone else's money is the root of all evil.

27. The liberal policy to simplify the tax form is to simply print money with their return address on it.
28. Liberals promise we will all be back on our feet. Sure, nobody can afford a car.
29. To live within my income I have to move to a poor neighborhood.
30. Liberals promised the economy would improve in the last quarter. Well, I'm down to my last quarter and it hasn't improved.
31. I feel real secure knowing that my bank account is protected by a government that is almost $20 trillion in debt.
32. The deficit proves one thing: Washington can't be trusted with a credit card.
33. I can still remember when the tip I now leave for lunch used to buy it.
34. If people would profit from their mistakes, we'd have a glorious future.
35. They crossed a mink with a gorilla for a cheaper mink coat, but the sleeves were too long.
36. A million dollars is spending $1,000 per day for three years. A billion is spending $1,000 per day for 3,000 years. A million is $1,000 bills stacked tightly on top of each other would create a stack four inches high. A billion dollars is $,1000 bills creating a stack 300 feet high. A trillion is $1,000 bills creating a stack 64 miles high. A trillion dollars laid end to end would reach 96 million miles.
37. Whenever anyone says, "It's only money," You can be sure it's your money they're talking about.
38. When it's time to check into a nursing home, wouldn't it be nice to own it?

39. I have decided that the reason the average family doesn't own a rhinoceros is because they have never been offered one for no money down and the balance in easy monthly payments.
40. I tried to get my family to approve a balanced budget but couldn't get a two-thirds majority.
41. One of the most difficult things any man can do is make ten easy payments.
42. Texan: "My wife made a millionaire out of me." "What were you before?" " A multi-millionaire."
43. Make money your God and it will plague you like the devil.
44. The trouble with being poor is it takes up all your time.
45. Too many people spend money they don't have, to buy things they don't need, to impress people they don't like.
46. That's nothing, "My grandfather came here with nothing more than a knapsack on the end of a stick, and the clothes on his back and became a multi-millionaire in mere months." What was in the knapsack? "A couple of million and another few million in foreign security stocks. It's always nice to have a little seed money."
47. After I paid my taxes my wallet was declared legally dead.
48. If women didn't exist money would have no meaning.
    Aristotle Onassis Greek shipping magnate

MORALITY

1. America seems to be in a moral freefall. It's like the government is giving us a tour through the sewer in a glass bottom boat.

NUDISTS

1. Two nudists broke up because they were seeing too much of each other.
2. The Supreme Court said nudists aren't covered by the first amendment, but they're not covered by anything.
3. They say they join nudist camps for sunshine and health. If that's true how come there aren't any blind nudists?
4. A family was bicycling past a nudist camp when out of the brush came several nudists biking ahead of them. One of the kids said, "Look Daddy, they don't have any helmets on."
5. Research has shown nudists are very ineffective people.
6. I feel like the mosquito that flew into a nudist camp. He surveyed the situation and said, "The opportunities here are so vast, I hardly know where to start."
7. Why it is that nudists are always the kind of people you would never want to see nude?

NUTRITION

1. So I went on the Vaudeville diet: I only eat food that gets thrown at me.
2. I started jogging but kept running into restaurants.
3. For a long time fat people have been the butt of jokes. In fact, they've been the big butts of jokes.
4. You are what you eat. Too many people must be eating nuts.
5. When it comes to dieting, moderation is the key. That's why I limit the number of diets I go on.

OBAMA

1. Why did Obama cross the road? He actually didn't, he just promised he would.
2. Q: Why do you play so much golf? Obama: "It keeps me fit." Q: "For what?" Obama: "Golf."
3. When Obama was born, even his parents ran away from home.

PATRIOTISM

1. If people want to claim the right to burn the American flag, I should have the right to do what I want with the flag pole.
2. My parents were very patriotic ; they laid down the stripes and we saw the stars.
3. Our only tanning booth was the woodshed.
4. Protesting Iraq citizens have been burning the American flag, so it looks like they're ready for democracy after all.
5. The average basketball fan knows the line ups of all the teams and about half the words of "The Star-Spangled Banner."

PENTAGON

1. Sign on Pentagon worker's desk: The secrecy of my job does not permit me to know what I'm doing.

POLITICS

1. Poly means "many" and tics are those things that suck blood out of you.
2. Truman said, "If you need a friend in Washington, get a dog."
3. I have come to the conclusion that politics is too serious a matter to be left to the politicians.
   Charles De Gaulle
4. Since a politician never believes what he says, he is always astonished when others do.
   Charles De Gaulle
5. Politicians offer yesterday's answers to tomorrow's problems
6. Government is not the solution to the problem; government is the problem.
   Ronald Reagan
7. The vice president is a spare tire on the automobile of government.
8. We've come a long way in 200 years; from George Washington who could not tell a lie to thousands of politicians who can.
9. Research has now revealed that 90 percent of politicians were not breast fed. Even their mothers didn't trust them.
10. President Clinton said he's for a third party, and a fourth party and a fifth.

11. They have the support of CBS (Clinton Broadcasting System), and NBC (National Broadcasters for Clinton), and CNN (Clinton News Network), Slay the Nation, and Meet the Depressed, and the NEA (National Extortion Association) and the ACLU (American Communist Lawyers Union or the Anti-Christian Liberties Union).

12. Too many politicians are like Christopher Columbus who went, and didn't know where he was going. When he got there, he didn't know where he was. And when he returned he didn't know where he had been. And he did it all on borrowed money.

13. The secret in politics is to keep the people who hate you away from the undecided.

14. A guy said to me the other day, "I wouldn't vote for you if you were Saint Peter." I said, "Sir, if I were Saint Peter, I wouldn't need your vote because you wouldn't be in my district."

15. When you hear political speeches you realize that America is still the land of promise.

16. Some candidates said they heard the call. They must be ventriloquists.

17. He said, "Most people who are as attractive, witty and intelligent as I am are conceited."

18. A successful politician is a guy who can delegate all the responsibility, shift all the blame, and appropriate all the credit.

19. You could say he's humble, unassuming and modest. You'd be wrong, but you could say that.

20. He has more talent in his little finger than in his big finger.

21. Give a politician enough rope and he'll hang you.
22. There are three kinds of politicians: The anointed, the appointed, and the disappointing.
23. He's a politician who stands on his record because if he ever steps off of it people may read it.
24. One senator to another: "Will you give your word of honor you will support my bill?" "Joe, I can't do that but I will give you my promise."
25. PACS are when the door to the politician's office is coin operated.
26. The main reason he went into politics was to meet women.
27. The main reason he went into politics was because it was all indoors and no heavy lifting.
28. A statesman is a politician who never got caught.
29. A statesman is a dead politician
30. When the roll is called up yonder he'll abstain.
31. At least he's the only politician I know who's incapable of a sex scandal.
32. I'm done celebrating New Year's eve. Rooms filled with balloons, noisemakers, and people wearing funny hats. I had enough of that during campaigns.
33. Politicians who don't know which way is up, raise taxes which don't know which way is down.
34. Politicians are trying to unite all the voters who are really serious about being undecided.
35. Indecision is a decision not to decide.
36. It's hard to have your finger on the problem when you're always holding it to the wind.
37. Politicians are like brooks: the shallow ones battle the loudest

38. It is the job of the media to look at every politician with a microscope. But for my opponent they should use proctoscope.

39. It makes me nervous when he says he wants to get back on track, knowing he has a one track mind.

40. Politics is the second oldest profession and it bears gross similarities to the first.

41. If the Lord helps those who help themselves, politicians have a powerful ally.

42. There is something you can do about junk mail. Write to your congressmen and tell them to stop sending it.

43. A congressman said, "I don't know why everyone's picking on me. I haven't done anything."

44. Politicians spend half their time making promises and the other half making excuses.

45. He's as good as his word as long as he doesn't talk too much.

46. All I know is what the politicians deny.

47. His speeches are like hash. He puts everything into them.

48. Mount Rushmore isn't the only place where politicians have rocks in their heads.

49. To raise our hopes, lower our taxes.

50. Politicians may not promise a rose garden, but they sure deliver the fertilizer.

51. Nowadays you rent a tuxedo for $150, your wife wears a $5,000 dress, and you go to a $5,000 per plate dinner all to elect a two-bit politician.

52. A cannibal rushed into the village and spread the word that a hunting party had just captured a

politician. One cannibal responded enthusiastically "Good, I've never tried a baloney sandwich."

53. He said he's a self-made man and I admire his willingness to take the blame.

54. Did you see the movie *Dave*? It's about a goofy guy who pretends to be President of the United States. Seems to me it would have been a lot more realistic if he had been named, Barack.

55. Don't you hate it when your air conditioner starts campaigning and blows nothing but hot air?

56. Two hundred and twenty years ago the US declared independence from Great Britain. Thank goodness, otherwise Queen Elizabeth would be running the country instead of Queen Hillary.

57. The great mosquito festival begins in Clute, Texas. It's the only event honoring blood-sucking pests that are not after campaign contributions.

58. The curly wigs our forefathers wore aren't needed anymore. Today, taxes and regulations will curl your hair.

59. A person with a lot of conviction will either be a tremendous success or end up in jail.

60. How many politicians does it take to grease a combine? Fourteen, if you put them through very slowly.

61. It's hard to roll up our sleeves to pay off the national debt when the government has just taken the shirt off our backs.

62. Blessed are the young, for they shall inherit the national debt.

63. Too many politicians are like bananas. The come in green, turn yellow, and leave rotten.

POST OFFICE

1. Obamacare promises to have the compassion of the IRS and the efficiency of the Post Office. That's why they put the FDA (Fraud and Drudge Abomination) in charge. Everyone gets the $50 pill.
2. How many congressmen does it take to mail a letter? Four. One to hold the letter, one to lick the stamp, one to head up the committee to investigate the mailbox, and the last to empty its contents of anything of value.
3. The cost of postage stamps is going up. You know what a box of 351 ammo costs?
4. The phone booth was invented in 1959, which was great because before then Superman had to change his clothes in the Post Office.

POVERTY

1. When I was a kid we were poor, but the government didn't have an agency to come and tell us we were poor.
2. There was a time when 99.5 percent of all American people were poor. This country wasn't settled by rich people. Many indentured themselves into slavery to get third-class steerage on a boat.
3. The pastor said, "It's like a shepherd with his sheep, and what does a shepherd do with his sheep?" Little Johnny raised his hand and said, "He shears them."
4. A friend of mine finally saved up enough money to purchase a cemetery plot. He had enough left over to take a cruise but he was lost at sea.
5. The role of government is to be a watchdog to be fed, not a cow to be milked.

PRAYER

1. Thank God for unanswered prayers. If God had answered all my prayers I would have married someone else.
Ruth Bell Graham, wife of Billy Graham

PRESIDENT

1. The president's team is well-balanced. They have problems everywhere.
2. His success has depended on his ability to go to the depths of sincerity whether he means it or not.

READING

1. I can't imagine a man really enjoying a book and reading it only once.
   C.S. Lewis
2. I cannot live without books.
   Thomas Jefferson
3. I would be most content if my children considered decorating as building as many book shelves as they can.

REAGAN

1. Some have forgotten why we have a military. It's not to promote war. It's to be prepared for peace.
2. I've always thought that the common sense and wisdom of government were summed up in a sign they used to have hanging over that gigantic Hoover Dam. It said, "Government property, do not remove."
3. Federal grants are like rabbits – they multiply like crazy, and when they're out you can't catch them.
4. There is no better way to establish hope for the future than to enlighten young minds.
5. Since I came to the White House, I got two hearing aids, a colon operation, skin cancer, a prostate operation, and I was shot. The dam thing is, I've never felt better in my life.
6. Being president is a lot like running a cemetery. You have a lot of people under you, but nobody is listening.
7. The West will not contain communism; it will transcend communism.
8. We don't celebrate Dependence on Government day on July 4th; we celebrate INDEPENDENCE DAY.
9. We don't have a $19 trillion debt because we haven't been taxed enough. We have a $19 trillion dollar debt because government spends too much.

10. While I take inspiration from the past, I live for the future.
11. We have long since discovered that nothing lasts longer than a temporary government program.
12. Wouldn't it be better for the human spirit and for the soul of this nation to encourage people to accept more responsibility to care for each other rather than leaving those tasks to paid bureaucrats?
13. We have a duty to protect the lives of the unborn.
14. We have every right to dream heroic dreams.
15. We Americans make no secret of our belief in freedom.
16. We the people get to tell the government what to do; it doesn't tell us.
17. The person who pays an ounce of principle for a pound of popularity gets badly cheated.

RELIGION

1. Only confession breaks the bind of sin that keeps us from heaven.
2. Many people will be asking their preacher in hell, "Why didn't you preach that what I was doing was sin?"

RIGHT TO DIE

1. The right to die movement is the next big craze. Hospitals will have an addition called the Marriott Monoxide or "The Holiday Is Over."
2. They will have a special feature: When you're checking in, you're checking out.
3. They are recruiting the next Dr. Kevorkian but he was not available for comment. He was on vacation at the Dead Sea.
4. He's a man about town. Unfortunately the town is "Death Valley."
5. He wants to run for Congress and he may win if he doesn't have too many skeletons in his closet.
6. His famous pick up line was, "Can I buy you one last drink?"
7. A guy in the hospital said to his mother "I need to take a nap, watch my plugs."
8. When Dr. Kevorkian went to jail it did help prison overcrowding.
9. I don't know why he started in Los Angeles. With O. J., drug gangs, killer bees, earthquakes, the Menendez Brothers, and the Night Stalker, It's the one state where there's a lot of competition.
10. He finally retired; said he would always quit when it quit being fun.

11. Dr. Kevorkian was sued once for malpractice. One of his patients lived.
12. He promised to cure every patient in one visit. Satisfaction or your mummy back.
13. His goal was to open a chain of suicide clinics to be bought out by a conglomerate.
14. Someone asked him, "How's business?" He said, "Dead."
15. To pay for Obamacare all we need is 10,000 Dr. Kevorkians.

RISK

1. To double your success rate, double your failure rate.
   Tom Watson
2. Too many people are thinking of security instead of opportunity. They seem more afraid of life than death.
   James F. Byrnes, American Politician
3. Allowing the government to run our pension plans and Social Security is like assigning a goat to guard a cabbage patch.
4. You can live on bland food to avoid ulcers, drink no coffee, not smoke, get eight hours of sleep per night, exercise, eat right, and die of Radon gas.

SINCERITY

1. The lions that ate the Christians were sincere. You have to be sincere about what's right.

SLAVERY

1. They set the slave free, striking off his chains. Then he was as much of a slave as ever. He was still bound to servility. He was still bound by fear and superstition, by ignorance, suspicion, and savagery. His slavery was not in chains, but in himself. They can only set free men free, and there is no need for that. Free men set themselves free.

SMOKING

1. The third Marlboro Man is still alive, but his horse just died of second hand smoke.
2. I told my patient to quit smoking and he started chewing toothpicks. He died of Dutch Elm disease.
3. Who can forget those immortal words, "Give me your tired, your poor, your huddled masses yearning to breathe free." Words that should be over every non-smoking section in America?
4. A smoker is a croaker.
5. There is a revolving door in closets. The gays have come out and smokers have gone in.

SOCIAL SECURITY

1. The way they're talking about Social Security, pretty soon the best retirement gift will be a job.
2. Have you noticed how the perception of Social Security is changing? It's gone from insurance, to entitlement, to handout.

SOCIALISM

1. They don't sell smile buttons in communist countries.
2. We would have been a lot better off if Groucho Marx had written *The Communist Manifesto* rather than Karl.
3. If we socialized the Sahara desert, in two years we'd be importing sand.
   Ronald Reagan
4. Socialism only works in two places: Heaven, where they don't need it, and Hell, where they already have it.
   Winston Churchill
5. The function of socialism is to raise suffering to a higher level.
   Normal Mailer, American Novelist, Playwright
6. The devil said to the Lord, "Give me your soul and I'll give you the world." Socialists say, "Give us your money and we will give you security from the cradle to the grave, womb to the tomb, basket to the casket." The only problem is maximum security is a prison. You can have four walls around you and they feed you three times per day but you're not free.
7. To train an elephant, they start when it's a baby and tie a huge log chain to its leg and to a large tree

trunk. The elephant tugs and pulls until it gives up. Finally, as soon as the elephant feels a pull on his leg, even when it's a small rope tied to a stake in the ground, it won't try to break loose because it has been conditioned to live in bondage.

8. Capitalism is the unequal distribution of blessings. Socialism is the equal distribution of misery.

9. Under communism if you have two cows the government shoots you and takes your cows. Under socialism the government takes one of your cows and leaves you just enough milk from the other cow to survive. Under capitalism if you have two cows you can sell one and get a bull.

10. In Canada if you're over age 55 and if a doctor finds out you have cancer and thinks you have six months to live, your next appointment is in nine months. If you die waiting for care, it's a tremendous cost savings.

11. Last year there were over 260 million prescriptions for Oxycontin despite the fact that there hasn't been one proven case of Oxycontin deficiency.

12. The FDA (Fraud and Drudge Abomination) is in charge of most of Obamacare.

13. By gnawing through a dike, even a rat may drown a nation.
Edmund Burke, Irish Statesman

SPACE TRAVEL

1. The trip to Mars includes a temperature of 150 degrees, severe earthquakes, and flooding. In other words, it's just like Los Angeles, without the crime and traffic.
2. I think it's important to invest in outer space. The further away you get, the smaller our government looks.

Ronald Reagan

SPEAKING

1. He can compress the most words into the smallest ideas of any man I ever met.
   Abraham Lincoln
2. It's not easy to reshape society in an after dinner speech.
   Winston Churchill
3. Blessed is the man who, having nothing to say, abstains from giving wordy evidence of that fact.
   George Eliot
4. If you yawn I will consider that a silent shout.
5. I'm an optimistic speaker. If I see people with their heads down and eyes closed I just assume they're praying for me to go on.
6. The right to be heard doesn't necessarily mean the right to be taken seriously.
   Hubert H. Humphrey, Jr, American Politician
7. Nothing confuses a political statement more than its clarification.
8. I didn't really say everything I said.
   Yogi Berra, American Baseball Player
9. It's important to have the gift of gab but he needs to know when to wrap it up.
10. His slogan should be: I came, I saw, I confused.
11. His political speech would have been perfect if only he had ended with: "But seriously folks."

12. You've heard of some speakers who need no introduction. Well, this speaker needs all the introduction he can get.
13. That was a tremendous sermon, pastor. You interrupted my train of thought a half a dozen times.
14. They only gave me five minutes to speak. That's OK; I haven't finished a speech in my life anyway.
15. If the microphone doesn't work: "Ladies and gentlemen, I want you to know I'm giving this speech free. What I'm charging for is the use of this equipment."
16. A woman said to me, "Every speech you give is better than the next."
17. He's a great speaker. I could hear him above all the snoring.
18. It bothers me when people say about a politician: "He's got a great delivery." So does Domino's Pizza; but we don't send them to the White House.
19. The president always gives a speech more than an hour long. George Washington never spoke more than 10 minutes. That's because presidents weren't allowed to lie back then.
20. Nothing is more frustrating than when someone goes right on talking when you're trying to interrupt.
21. Poise is the ability to go right on talking while the other guy picks up the check.
22. I'd a heap rather hear a man say, "I seen" when he saw something than to say, "I saw" when he ain't seen nothing.
Ernest Bevin, British Statesman

23. The last time I spoke I didn't get a standing ovation, but some of the people who were walking out waved.
24. One time I got a crouching ovation. That's when a guy leans forward to stand up and looks around and nobody else wants to stand so he sits back down.
25. Plant your feet on the right place, then stand firm. **Abraham Lincoln**
26. It's better to be hated for telling the truth than to be loved for telling a lie.

SPIN

1. My congressman got angry when I said he was dishonest. He said he was not dishonest. He was just ethically challenged.
2. It's no longer called lying. It's a temporary lapse in memory.
3. When Bill Clinton was guilty of lying to the American public, lying to a grand jury, obstruction of justice, and bombing an aspirin factory to divert the attention away from the testimony of Monica Lewinsky he was impeached. He held a press conference and considered it a badge of honor, and ever since, the movie *Wag the Dog* has been the chief reference of liberal politicians, Republican or Democrat.
4. When Russia played the United States in soccer, the U.S. won. The next day in the Russian paper it said, "Russia comes in second. The United States comes in next to last."
5. I'm happy to report there is a speed up of the slow down and there is no downturn of the upturn, but things are getting worse slower.

STATESMAN

1. We never appreciated Harry Truman until he was dead. We can hardly wait to apply the same principle to other politicians.
2. A man of stature doesn't need status.
3. In Washington those who travel the high road of humility are not bothered by heavy traffic.
   Alan K. Simpson(R-WY)

SUCCESS

1. The man who makes every minute count is the man of the hour.
2. Nobody has ever climbed the ladder of success with his hands in his pockets.
3. He who hesitates is sometimes saved.
4. The world is not interested in the storms you've encountered, but whether you brought in the ship.
5. A well-adjusted person is one who can make the same mistake twice without getting nervous.
6. A successful person can go from failure to failure with no loss of enthusiasm.
    Winston Churchill
7. The bottom line is not always a top priority.
8. When people start criticizing your mistakes you know you're making high quality mistakes.
    Frank A. Clark, American politician, The Country Parson
9. If it's lonely at the top it's only because your relatives haven't discovered you're there yet.
10. Those who keep an orderly desk will never know the thrill of finding something they thought was irretrievably lost.
11. If at first you don't succeed, failure may be your thing.
12. If at first you don't succeed, try second base.

TAXES

1. I'm proud to pay my taxes, but I could be just as proud for half as much.
2. To raise our hopes, lower our taxes.
3. I have plenty of money for taxes. Its food clothing and shelter I'm struggling with.
4. If the government doesn't get off our backs, the whole country will need a chiropractor.
5. What goes up must come down; except for taxes.
6. The president should star in a new movie for the American taxpayer. We'd call it *Numb and Number*.
7. The government comes up with the ways and leaves the means to the taxpayer.
8. It's hard to roll up your sleeves to make a living when the government takes the shirt off your back.
9. The government has now approved of the IRS taking credit cards to pay our taxes. What a novel idea. Borrowing money to pay off debt. Will the government approve of such a creative idea?
10. I am philosophically opposed to any tax increase... That does not mean I will not support one.
    Bill Clinton
11. It's income tax time again when we find out we can get wounded by a blank.
12. Doing your own taxes is like "do it yourself mugging."

13. I sent the IRS a quart of blood and they said they prefer to think they got the last drop.
14. We are born free and taxed to death.
15. At least the weather warms up about the time the government takes the shirt off our backs.
16. Filling out income tax is like a girl going to the beach. Both take off as much as the law will allow.
17. A guy wrote to the IRS and thanked them for his refund. That's like thanking a mugger for letting you keep your watch.
18. I have good news and bad news. The good news is my house is worth $50,000 more. The bad news is the tax assessor told me.
19. One guy was so rich that when he got sick, the IRS sent him a get well card.
20. Abraham Lincoln said, "You can fool some of the people all of the time, and all of the people some of the time." He of course never saw the new tax form.
21. April 15th is Easter and April 16th is the tax deadline. One day eggs get rolled and the next day we do.
22. Liberals have taxed everything except their memory.
23. Why does a slight tax increase cost you $200 but a substantial tax decrease save you 30 cents?
24. We have taxed our economy the same way old time doctors bled their patients; and with similar results. **Governor William F. Weld (R-MA)**
25. Did you ever wonder if taxation without representation might have been cheaper? **Eugene McCarthy**
26. The taxes we have today, with representation, make King George look like a piker.

27. The difference between death and taxes is, death doesn't get worse every time Congress convenes.

28. Never underestimate the ability of Democrats to wet their finger and hold it to the wind.

29. I've been waiting so long for my ship to come in that my pier collapsed.

30. It's tax time again; have you hugged your wallet today?

31. Let's face it. If God really wanted us to be solvent, He would never have allowed the IRS.

32. I think we should spell it TAXX. If anything deserves to be a four letter word this is it.

33. Winning isn't everything. The tax people take a huge chunk of it.

34. Isn't it sneaky how they call it a tax return? It's as if your money was going to make a round trip.

35. Birth control pills are deductible; but only if they don't work.

36. If Patrick Henry thought taxation without representation was bad, he should see it with representation.

37. The trouble with politics is too many people with half a mind to run do so.

38. Tax comes from the Latin word *taxares,* which means "To touch sharply."

39. A taxpayer is the Incomepoop of the Year.

40. Doing your own taxes is like "Do it yourself mugging."

41. As far as I'm concerned all tax preparation is H.

42. I'm a member of the CIO. Everybody I C I owe.

43. Why don't you pay your taxes with a smile? I wish I could but they prefer cash.

44. Now they tell us you don't have to fill out income tax forms if you've been dead a year or longer.

45. We owe a lot to the IRS; ulcers, nausea, and diarrhea.

46. Now the IRS is selling gift certificates.

47. An IRS agent is writing a book entitled, *How I made 1.8 million dollars from the guy who wrote a book about making 2 million dollars in the stock market.*

48. CPA stands for Constant Pain in the Rear.

49. Let us prepare your taxes and save you time; like 5 to 10 years.

50. The biggest job Congress has is how to get the money from the taxpayer without disturbing the votes.

51. Thirty percent approve of the president's tax plan. The rest of the people have jobs.

52. They say the devil is in the details. I wonder if he does tax returns!

53. Liberal agenda: "Another quiet weekend of taxing and spending."

54. Washington DC is both the crime capital and the seat of government. Isn't this redundant?

55. My wife knows nothing about football. She thinks a quarterback is a tax refund.

56. Nowadays when someone builds a better mousetrap, the government comes up with a better mouse.

57. Collecting more taxes than is absolutely necessary is legalized robbery.
Calvin Coolidge

58. The taxpayer is the only animal that can be skinned more than once.

59. It's hard to believe that historians are trying to convince us this country was founded partly to avoid taxation.

60. We should be able to invest in taxes. It's the one thing that's guaranteed to go up.

61. I always procrastinate and pay my 1040 at 10:40 on April 15th.

62. There's a section in the IRS tax form that says, "Do not write below this space." Every once in a while someone scribbles in bold red ink, "I will write anywhere I darn please." As long as we have people like that there's still hope.

63. Too many people think everyone has the right to life, liberty and the pursuit of pension.

64. Ever notice why elections are November fourth, which is about as far away from July Fourth as you can get? If elections were on July Fourth, the taxpayers would be very mindful of the cost of government.

65. Too many politicians don't do any deep thinking until they put the country in a deep hole.

66. Taxpayer: Someone who has the Government on his payroll.

67. They asked Joe Lewis who hit him the hardest when he was boxing. He said, "That's easy, Uncle Sam."

68. The last tax relief act was 1,248 pages making ours the most complex tax law in history.

69. There's no such thing as a good tax.
Winston Churchill.

70. The new tax plan and budget is the fairest of them all. It will give everyone an equal chance at poverty and misery.
71. A statistician is someone who is good with numbers but doesn't have the personality to be an accountant.
72. Our nation needs a tax system that at least looks like it was something designed on purpose. At least when you make sausage you know the pig isn't coming back. When you use the short form the government gets your money. When you use the long form the accountant gets it.
73. Liberal promises of today are the taxes of tomorrow.

TAXPAYER'S POEM

I'm an ordinary taxpayer, the kind that bears the brunts.
I'm assigned to fight three heavy weights, all three of them at once.
Federal, state and local, each with the power to tax,
Are ganging up to cut me down, like woodsmen with an ax.
A Federal to the midriff, a local to the head,
The state tax drives me up the ropes, my arms and legs are dead.
I cannot block six fists at once, each blow is keenly felt.
I'm doubled up, half paralyzed,

From blows below the belt.
"Murder the bum," the planners scream,
The bureaucrats agree. I've a sickening feeling
knowing that
The bum they mean is me.
My crime is that I like to work, and profit from
my labors.
They heard me say, "Don't loot my pay, and
throw it at my neighbors."
But in the early light of dawn, called truth will
stun these sages,
For they'll find the bum whose death they
cheered,
Was the bum who paid their wages.

TEA PARTY

1. Tea Party wants to screw the country. It's a racist thing. It's unnerving seeing the Tea Party getting such traction. It just shows the weak, dark underside of America. It's racist.

   Morgan Freeman, Actor

2. Tea Party people are terrorists.

   Joe Biden

3. Tea Party can just go to hell.

   Maxine Waters (D-CA)

4. The Tea Party rally consisted of 1.9 million hard working Americans that went to Washington on their own time, on their own dime for only one reason; Love of country. After the rally, there wasn't as much as a gum wrapper on the streets. Not one story in the Lame Stream Media nor a picture of the rally.

TERM LIMITS

1. Americans now have realized that we must have term limits, with maybe some time off for good behavior.

TERRORISM

1. We must deal strongly with terrorist organizations. I mean it's about time we get tough with the IRS.

THINKING

1. Men simply don't take the time to think.
   Albert Schweitzer
2. Great spirits have always encountered violent opposition from mediocre minds.
   Albert Einstein
3. When you're all by yourself are you in good company?
4. Only the shallow know themselves.
5. My inferiority complexes are not as good as yours.
6. Once you expand your mind, it never returns to its former size.
7. The brain is an organ in which we think that we think.
8. Some political candidates are starting to have second thoughts. Others are still trying to come up with their first.
9. The hardest thing in the world to understand is the income tax code.
   Albert Einstein
10. What luck for rulers that men do not think.
    Adolf Hitler
11. Liberals have thought about how to tax people's thinking. However they have exempted themselves by how they define it.
12. The Lord's Prayer is 56 words, Lincoln's Gettysburg address is 266 words. The Ten Commandments are

297 words and the Declaration of Independence is 300 words. But a new government order on the price of cabbage is 26,911 words. We have 10,000 laws to enforce the Ten Commandments. The tax code is 78,000 pages. Now that's something to think about!

13. If a man is bald in front he's a thinker. If he's bald in back, he's sexy. If he's bald both places, he thinks he's sexy.

14. The first man to make a mountain out of a molehill was a real estate agent.

15. The beginning of wisdom is the realization that the thing you are anxious about today won't seem important tomorrow.

16. Curiosity is the first rung on the ladder of learning.

17. Too often we don't ask our students to think, but only to learn the results of other people's thinking.
   Don Robinson

18. Just because you're not paranoid doesn't mean they're not out to get you.

19. The average person really doesn't do any deep thinking until he gets in a hole.

20. There aren't enough crutches in the world for all the lame excuses.

TOLERANCE

1. The trouble with being tolerant is that people think you don't understand the problem.
2. Tolerance is the last virtue of a decadent society.
   C. S. Lewis
3. Thanks to rock music nobody has to live a life of quiet desperation.
4. I hate intolerant people.

TRUTH

1. If 50 million people say a foolish thing it is still a foolish thing.
   Anatole France, French Poet, Novelist
2. In God we trust; all others must pay cash.
3. We believe in truth in advertising: We honor all major credit cards. Some we adore.
4. The president needs a TV show: *Truth or No Consequences.*
5. With all the talk of shredding, I can see why God gave us the Ten Commandments on stone.
6. Right is right no matter if nobody is right; wrong is wrong, no matter if everybody is wrong.
   Bishop Fulton Sheen
7. The trouble with stretching the truth is sometimes it snaps back.
8. Politician - Practice makes perfect. If you tell a lie, always rehearse it. If it doesn't sound good to you, it won't sound good to anybody.
9. Speak softly, some people believe anything if you whisper it to them.
10. You don't have to tell deliberate lies, but sometimes you have to be evasive.
11. Rather than love, money or fame, give me truth.
    Henry David Thoreau, American Author, Abolitionist

12. Witness on the stand to presiding judge: "I swore to tell the truth but every time I try, some lawyer objects."

13. Most people at some time stumble over the truth, but most pick themselves up, brush themselves off and walk away as if nothing had happened."
Winston Churchill.

14. Trust your instincts. If you have no instincts, trust your impulses.
Tammy Grimes, American Actress, Singer

15. What is moral is anything you feel good after.
Ernest Hemmingway – He committed suicide

16. God seems to have left the receiver off the hook.

17. Lawyer to Clinton when he was under oath: "Please answer the question yes or no. Not, 'Would I lie to you?'"

18. It's annoying to be honest to no purpose.
Ovid, Roman Poet

19. Some people claim to be ethical, when all they really are is afraid of being caught. As an anonymous observer noted, "Conscience gets a lot of credit that belongs to cold feet."

20. I try not to break the rules, just to test their elasticity.
Bill Veeck, American Baseball Executive

21. For every report there is an equal and opposite expert to refute it.

22. Character is what you do on the third and fourth tries.
James Michener, Author

23. Fiction is obliged to stick to possibilities. Truth isn't.
Mark Twain

24. Truth is shorter than fiction.
    Irving Cohen
25. Under current law, it is a crime for a private citizen to lie to a government official, but not for the government official to lie to the people.
    Donald M. Fraser(D-MN)
26. As scarce as truth is, the supply has always been in excess of the demand.
    Josh Billings, Humorist, Lecturer
27. One of the most striking differences between a cat and a lie is that a cat has only nine lives.
    Mark Twain
28. There are only two ways of telling the complete truth - anonymously and posthumously.
    Thomas Sowell
29. Actions lie louder than words.
30. In order to preserve your self-respect, it is sometimes necessary to lie and cheat.
    Robert Byrne, Author
31. It's always the best policy to tell the truth, unless, of course, you are an exceptionally good liar.
    Jerome K. Jerome, Author, Humorist
32. A lie can travel halfway around the world while the truth is putting its shoes on.
    Mark Twain
33. Living without a conscience is like driving a car without the brakes on.
    Budd Shulberg, American Screenwriter, Novelist
34. If you lose your conscience, you have nothing else of value to lose.
35. A clear conscience is often the sign of a bad memory.
    Anonymous

36. The other day he called a spade a spade, and later issued a retraction.

37. He has mastered the art of making whole lies out of half-truths.

38. Last night I slept like a Democrat. First I lied on one side and then I lied on the other.

39. The days are exciting and inspiring, but like Solomon, who was given the choice to ask for anything, our politicians and the American people need to ask for wisdom.

40. Where does a certified pathological liar go to get certified?

41. Why would I lie about my opponent when the truth is bad enough?

42. "I didn't think the rules applied to me!" Tiger Woods said in his apology after about the ninth bimbo came forward with a love child. What rules? The moral laws of the universe apply to everyone, everywhere, all the time. Making about $100 million per month, having a beautiful wife and kids wasn't enough. I have money, power, fame and fortune. I can do anything I want. But like Solomon – who said, "Vanity of vanities, it's all vanity, it's like chasing the wind. It doesn't satisfy the soul."

43. One man armed with truth is an army; one man with God is a majority.

44. No law is just that does not comport with the moral laws of God.
    Martin Luther King Jr.

45. New study on *Brietbart News*: Sexual orientation is not biological.

UNEMPLOYMENT

1. If you ask me, one of the country's biggest problems is the large number of the unemployed still on the payroll.
2. What this country needs is more unemployed politicians.
3. Times are tough. The guy in front of me in line at the unemployment office is the same guy who laid me off in my last job.
4. And what are your expectations asked the owner of a company to an applicant. "I'd like to start at $75,000 per year, have three weeks' paid vacation, paid holidays, and good opportunity for advancement. The employer said, "Yes, why in addition to that we provide full health insurance, dental, two weeks sick leave, and a new car." The applicant said, "You're kidding." The owner said, "Of course I am, but you started it."
5. Sign on company door: IF YOU ARE NOT FIRED WITH ENTHUSIASM, YOU WILL BE FIRED WITH ENTHUSIASM.